How to Sell a House Fast in a Slow Real Estate Market

How to Sell a House Fast in a Slow Real Estate Market

A 30-Day Plan For Motivated Sellers

WILLIAM BRONCHICK, ESQ.
RAY COOPER

John Wiley & Sons, Inc.

Published by John Wiley & Sons, Inc., Hoboken, New Jersey
Published simultaneously in Canada

For general information on our other products and services or for technical support, please contact our Customer Care Department within the United States at (800) 762-2974, outside the United States at (317) 572-3993 or fax (317) 572-4002.

Wiley also publishes its books in a variety of electronic formats. Some content that appears in print may not be available in electronic books. For more information about Wiley products, visit our web site at www.wiley.com.

Library of Congress Cataloging-in-Publication Data:

Bronchick, William.
    How to sell a house fast in a slow real estate market : a 30-day plan
for motivated sellers / William Bronchick, Ray Cooper.
        p. cm.
    Includes index.
    ISBN 978-0-470-38260-8 (pbk.)
    1. House selling. I. cooper, Ray, 1965- II. Title.
    HD1390.5.b765   2009
    643'.12–dc22
                                                        2008018569
Printed in the United States of America.

10 9 8 7 6 5 4 3 2 1

CONTENTS

This book explains a somewhat unorthodox, yet highly effective system for selling your house quickly and for the highest possible price in a slow market. The strategies and techniques in this book have been tested and honed thousands of times in two decades of market cycles. They have helped countless homeowners, investors, and professional real estate agents sell their houses quickly and for the highest possible price.

First, though we'd like to congratulate you for having the courage and the wisdom to invest your time and money in this book. You have made the decision to take the first step toward solving your house problem, which is the hardest step. You have the guts to be one of the 5 percent that actually are the "doers" in life, while the other 95 percent will sit back and wonder what has happened. You have also taken the first step toward putting more money in your pocket.

Of course, simply reading this book is not the solution to your problem. It's not the be all and end all. *You* are the solution to your problem, because *only you* can take what you learn and implement the strategies and techniques that will help you to sell your house, put many thousands of dollars in your pocket, and a big smile on your face for a job well done. We give you powerful tools. However, you must pick them up and use them at the right place and at the right time. You can do it!

Many of you need to sell your house fast—you want to be under contract in 30 days or less. Some of you may be holding vacant investment properties and making mortgage payments on two or more properties. You're seeing how quickly this will drain your bank account if you don't do something right now. No matter what your local market looks like, following the principles in this book will help you achieve your goal of selling your house fast.

A TYPICAL SUCCESS STORY—SELLING A HOUSE IN THE MIDDLE OF WINTER, IN A LOUSY MARKET

Greg is a good example of a success story. He and his wife recently sold their house, in an extremely slow market, in less than 30 days. How bad was it? In Greg's town, there were 418 houses for sale, and only 40 that had closed in the last month. Normally under these terrible conditions it would take six months or more to sell a house—even at a reasonable price. Greg and his wife followed our advice and prepared their home for sale by first having the house professionally inspected for obvious defects (see Chapter 2). Second, they did their due diligence and very carefully studied the direct competition to their home and the homes that had recently sold (see Chapter 2). They knew that their home was worth not less than $600,000 and not more than $650,000 in a stable market. Because they were very motivated and serious sellers and could not afford to wait 6 to 12 months to sell, they decided to use some of the strategies we will later discuss, including the price range listing (see Chapter 3). The ultimate selling price was $625,000, which was well within their estimated range. This price range represents the highest range of the town (top 5 percent), yet still Greg and his wife were able to sell their house quickly, in the middle of the winter, in a down market. Under these circumstances, it's easy for homeowners to feel helpless. The main reason this house sold so quickly was because Greg and his wife took immediate action, made no excuses, and implemented the strategies we outline in this book.

Time is of the essence for you—no excuses, no delays. You must be willing to commit to marketing and selling your house for the next three to six to eight weeks. It will take some work and some effort on your part, but the increased profit to you will be well worth it. The time you invest in preparing and marketing for the open house will pay you back many times more than your current profession. Imagine investing a few weekends of your time to make an extra 10 percent on the sale of your property; this time translates into an hourly wage of more than $1,000 an hour!

For those of you who are not under any immediate pressure, but are thinking about selling your house a few months from now, you also need to commit to doing what's necessary to reach your goal, but you have more time to do the things that are necessary to get your house priced-ranged effectively and ready to sell itself.

In Chapter 1, we discuss the foundation of our success principles: the right attitude. You can't manage what you can't measure, so you must take a measurement of your local home-selling marketplace. In Chapter 2, you learn how to research your market, including the all-important comp book.

Chapter 3 shows you the exact formula for determining how to sell your property quickly at the highest possible price.

Chapter 4 reveals how to get your home ready for sale, including the secrets of staging. You only get one chance to make the right first impression, so you will want to read this chapter twice.

Chapter 5 is a page from the football playbook—the best offense is a good defense. You learn how to organize your information to strike while the iron is hot.

Chapter 6 answers the all-important question of whether to use an agent or do it yourself. You learn how to sell it yourself and a revolutionary method to make sure if you do choose an agent, you find the best one to sell your house.

Chapter 7 explains how to finance the sale of your house in a New York minute, so your buyers don't have to deal with traditional banks.

Chapter 8 is all about driving customers to your open house by developing a killer marketing plan. You learn the "goose that lays the golden egg" principle that helps flush out the highest and best customer who is most likely to pay you the highest price.

In Chapter 9, you learn the secrets of effective negotiating so that you can convert offers to cash with the lowest risk of losing the deal.

Chapter 10 reveals how to employ an unusual, yet effective strategy for the hardest-to-sell house—the round robin auction. You learn how to get dozens of people through your house in one weekend bidding against each other for the right to make you an offer.

Chapter 11 deals with the difficult issue of having a house for which you owe more than it's worth. Your only practical option is a short sale, which is outlined in detail.

Chapter 12 outlines the strategies of this book and how to put them into action. Throughout the book, we also offer advanced tips for real estate professionals and investors.

At the moment, you may not see the light at the end of the tunnel. All you're hearing is talk about the weakening real estate market conditions. This is typical of market psychology when prices are down, and many people are overreacting. Eventually the brave veterans show the way to the next up cycle, which will *definitely* come again as it has in past market cycles. It's not a matter of if, just when. The first clue will be the housing supply quotient (see Chapter 2) turnaround, as it did in the mid 1990s, after a period of decline. Real estate markets tend to take the elevator down and the stairs up. But up they will go and go as the population invariably continues to climb and people in your area need a place to live.

Now, let's get ready to sell your house!

CHAPTER 1

Attitude Is Everything in a Down Market

Whether you think you can or you think you can't, you are right.

—Henry Ford

In any difficult housing market, most people who need to sell their property become convinced that their local market is hopeless. Instead of working harder to market their property, they sit back and suffer. This is why having a positive, proactive attitude is your best advantage in a highly competitive market. Some people reading this will argue that a positive attitude doesn't always work. Well, maybe not, but we know one thing for sure——negative thinking and a negative attitude *never* work! So your only choice and your only chance for success in this market are to stay positive and focus your energy on doing everything you can to sell your house. That's exactly what this book will help you do.

A History Lesson on Real Estate Cycles

If your housing market is bad, and you're desperate to sell your house, you need serious answers to your burning question, "How do I sell fast in a slow market?" We intend to answer this question in full detail, but first we need to give you some perspective on the housing market. About every 10 years, on average, real estate values tend to double in most major metropolitan areas. For example, in the 1920s, the original colonial homes sold for just under $2,500 in Long Island, New York. Since then, real estate prices have doubled almost 8 times over the last 80 years. That averages out to a 100 percent increase approximately every 10 years. An interesting note to this is that about every 10 years, real estate values must correct before they enter their next doubling cycle.

The real estate cycle is typically three steps forward and one step backwards—a 100 percent increase occurring in three steps of roughly 33 percent each.

In the last market cycle of the 1980s real estate values doubled, followed by a correction of the early 1990s, which equated to a 20 to 30 percent decrease over a three- to five-year period. This cycle was then followed by the postmillennium cycle boom of 100 percent from the last high point of the previous cycle. We are now in the naturally occurring phase of a correction, or downturn in the cycle. This essential and beneficial adjustment gives the market time to reflect and regather momentum and strength for the next doubling cycle. This has occurred time and time again because the long-term demand for housing is growing at an exponential rate. Population in the United States is expected to double by the end of the century according to the United States Census Bureau. This will continue to drive prices higher as it has for the last 100 years.

Since we know based on history that nearly all real estate prices will double again, it's not a matter of if your house will sell, it's a matter of *when*. Sharing this perspective with your prospective buyers will put them in the right frame of mind to buy now versus next year if they plan on staying in the home more than five years. If a buyer is apprehensive about whether this is the right time to invest, ask him if he'd like to buy his parent's home for the price they paid for it—the answer will be obviously yes, and your buyer will think carefully about the long-term value of your house as an investment.

Which Comes First, the Value of Your House or the Value of Your Time?

Assuming that you don't have three to five years to wait out the market in order to sell your house for top dollar, the next issue is this: What's more valuable to you, your time or the amount of money you get for your house? Most sellers in a down market forget that although they may be selling their house at a 10 to 20 percent discount over the price that they could have received a year or two ago, typically this very same discount will also apply to the next home they will buy. All ships rise and fall with the tides. In the case of the seller who is looking to trade up, these market conditions are absolutely ideal. This is the market that trade-up buyers should be dreaming of! If you are selling a $500,000 house for $400,000, you are sustaining a $100,000 loss. If you are buying a $1,000,000 replacement house for $800,000, you are saving $200,000, and thus gaining a net $100,000 in equity.

On the other hand, if you are moving down in price or are not going to purchase another home as a replacement, then you'd better price your house to sell or, if you can, wait out the market for the next cycle. If you have to sell and are not trading up, there are still important strategies such as owner financing that will yield you top dollar even in a soft market. We will explain this in Chapter 7.

You may be surprised to hear it from us, but holding out to get top dollar for your house is not the most important thing. The needs of your family, your job, and your lifestyle are all more important. We have counseled thousands of families and the common denominator is that the quality of their living arrangements will always trump the desire to get the absolute highest price. In other words, it may be better for you to take a little less for your house now and move into the house you really want than to hold out for full price and stay another year in a place you don't want.

How Many Buyers Does It Take to Sell a House?

How many buyers does it take to sell a house? The obvious answer is one. You need to keep this in mind when trying to sell a house in a market where conditions are bad for sellers. In a soft real estate market the numbers are not favorable to sellers, but you have to consider the numbers of prospective buyers you need to sell *your* house, not the market numbers in general.

In our experience the number of prospective buyers needed for selling a house play out to be 100-10-1. That is, you'll need 100 people considering your house to get 10 qualified buyers and 1 solid offer. This being the case, you need to do whatever it takes to get the numbers working in your favor to get your house sold. If you quit after 3 prospective buyers, you won't end up with the best possible offer on your house. You have to work with the 100-10-1 rule to get the most out of selling your house.

Maintain a Positive Attitude, Assuming a Negative Result

In *Winning Through Intimidation* (Fawcett 1984) author Robert Ringer talks about the importance of maintaining a positive attitude *combined with* the assumption of a negative result. In other words, Ringer suggests that you be prepared for the worst case scenario while at the same time putting your best foot forward to get the best possible result. This will take the mental pressure off you and allow you to focus on getting the job done. This approach, we believe, allows you to be positive and realistic in your mental assessment of selling your house.

Media Reporting on the Real Estate Market Is Biased

There's an old expression in the media business, "If it bleeds, it leads." In other words, the media loves to cover negative news more than positive because it sells better. When the real estate market is in turmoil, the media loves to run these negative headlines to keep reminding people how bad things are. When buyers hear the bad news, it affects demand because the negative news drives fear, which makes buyers worry about whether the time is right to buy a home.

Is the media simply reporting the news, or does the media actually affect the news in this regard? The answer is obviously both. The media's reporting negative news alone can't shape a real estate market. However, since perception is often reality, when buyers are spooked, they may shy away from buying. This affects lenders, builders, real estate agents and other professionals who rely on the real estate business for their income. Bad coverage almost becomes a self-fulfilling prophecy because things get worse and the media again reminds us how bad things are.

But, are things really as bad as the media reports? At the time of this printing (late 2008), the numbers certainly do reflect falling home prices and rising foreclosures. When you hear that foreclosures have doubled or even tripled in a particular area, this may sound catastrophic at first until you realize that the vast majority of homes (97 to 99 percent, depending on the local market) are not in foreclosure. Despite the doom and gloom, there's always a buyer for a well-kept home offered at the right price and terms. In short, don't read the paper if you want to keep a positive attitude and sell your home fast!

Ready Fire, Aim, Fire

Well done is better than well said—you have to take a whole lot of action to get your house sold. In a good real estate market, people can sell a house fast, so when things slow down, they figure, "Oh well, there's nothing I can do." Nothing could be further from the truth. Not only is there something you can do, but there's a lot you *must* do to get your house sold. However, it's not just about working hard, it's about working *smart*. You need to do things in the right order and in the right way to get the proper results. However, don't focus too much on perfection before you take action. You've probably seen C students who outperform A students in real life. This is because the C student is often satisfied with doing a mediocre job at something, just to get it done. The A student mentality often leads to paralysis of analysis and inaction. In other words, the bottom line is getting your house exposed to as many buyers as possible, not necessarily getting it done perfectly. For example, many sellers want to show their house only when it's convenient for them and the house is in perfect shape, instead of when a buyer is ready. While showing a house in its best condition is a priority, it doesn't make sense to put off a ready, willing and able buyer for too long.

Don't Be Cheap

This isn't the time to have short arms and deep pockets. Depending on the condition of your house and the checklist of things that you know you'll have to do in order to sell your house quickly, you must be willing to put out the initial investment and have the confidence to know your small out-of-pocket investment now will be returned to you many times over. Those of you who have maintained your house well over the years may only need to invest several hundred dollars. Obviously, those of you who have never put any money back into your house will have to invest more. It's like a burn. A third-degree burn is much more serious than a first degree burn and will require more attention and expense. If you're reading this and saying to yourself, "I don't have $500, or I don't have $2,000 to do the things I need to do," we urge you to change your thinking right now. You may say you can't afford it, but the bottom line is this—you can't afford not to do it.

If you have to borrow from a family member or friend or put it on your credit card to get it done, then do it. We all hate to borrow or put expenses on credit cards, but in a situation like this, we know the expense will allow you to sell your property quickly and for a lot more money. So you must adopt the attitude of full confidence that whatever you borrow or have advanced to you will be paid back in a very short period of time. If you have to borrow $5,000 to fix a property with more serious problems, then do it. If you have done your homework and due diligence, and your research tells you that a $5,000 investment in your house will allow you to sell your house quickly and for a $20,000 profit, or more, then it's a no-brainer. Sometimes you have to take one step back in order to take two steps forward. This is one of those times.

Use This Book as a Competitive Advantage

Lack of knowledge about what it takes to sell a house in a slow market is probably the single biggest disadvantage your competition has. That's why it's critical to use this book as a competitive weapon. Most people only have the opportunity to sell a few houses in their lifetime and often rely on professionals to do the work. Thus, the average home seller does not have enough practice to get really good at the job. In fact, most real estate agents who sell houses for a living are no really good at it. The top 5 percent of agents in any market do the vast majority of the business. Our experience in selling thousands of homes will give you the very specialized knowledge you'll need to get your house sold fast and at the highest price you can get for your market.

If you're trying to lose weight, you can eat less, exercise more, take supplements, drink plenty of water or get more sleep. The more of these you do, the faster you'll get to your goal. Likewise, there are dozens of effective tools you'll get from reading this book, and we recommend you employ as many as possible, so that you get the best results in the shortest period of time.

Excuses won't sell your house—preparedness and relentless action will!

Chapter Summary

- Attitude is everything—you can't sell a house if you don't have belief in yourself.
- Fear can be overcome by learning specialized knowledge.
- Give 100 percent, and don't make excuses.

CHAPTER 2

How to Research Your Competition and Learn Your Market

Give me six hours to chop down a tree and I'll spend the first four sharpening the axe.

—Abraham Lincoln

Most sellers make the colossal mistake of not knowing the facts about their market before proceeding with selling their home, which is why they fail miserably when the market is bad. One of the most important things you can do to get your house sold is to learn your market, the current value of your property and your competition. Most sellers operate in the dark, simply offering the property for the price they want, without regard to what other houses have sold for and are currently selling for. The danger of undervaluing or overpricing your home is that it can cost you tens of thousands of dollars. If it's priced too low, people may think something is wrong with it. If it's priced too high, nobody will be interested enough to make it through your front door. This chapter will reveal how to research effectively so you can set the price just right.

Knowledge Is Power

Sellers of real estate need to think in three dimensions. The first dimension is the overview or general tide of the market. The second is how your boat is sailing within that market. Third is the amount of time you have available to achieve the goal of selling your house. For example, if your prevailing local market conditions are such that the number of sellers far outweigh the number of buyers and you have only a month to get your house sold, then obviously great efforts and aggressive pricing, along with avoiding mistakes, will be necessary to get to the closing table quickly. Furthermore, if your property is like many others on the market and lacks uniqueness, then creativity and marketing outside the box, and physical improvements to the property may be necessary.

Let's say, as an example, that your market is flooded with two-bedroom homes competing with your house. It may be worthwhile to convert a family room or garage into another bedroom, assuming local zoning or building codes permit. Knowing the preference of buyers is key, when planning your approach to marketing the home. It's not about your likes, tastes and desires, but rather about what's hot and what's not.

Hiring a Home Inspector Will Give You a Competitive Advantage

It's common practice for buyers to hire a home inspector to do a complete and thorough inspection of the property. A smart seller will arrange for an inspection *prior* to showing the house to identify any latent defects that might kill a deal with a buyer. Furthermore, correcting safety issues will help eliminate any potential legal issues.

If you haven't already done so, hire a home inspector to give you a thorough inspection of the home. The American Society of Home Inspectors (www.ASHI.org) and the National Association of Home Inspectors (www.NAHI.org) are the best places to find a qualified home inspector. An inspector with a background in construction who can quote you ballpark figures for repairs is often the best choice.

Remember that the home inspector is qualified to inspect the home for items that don't conform to the current building standards.

He is also looking for defects in the systems and construction of the property, along with many other issues.

It is important to remember that home inspectors are not appraisers. They may be qualified to give estimates for cost of repairs, but the current market value of the property is something they are rarely qualified to speak about. In the early 1990s, we consulted on a home purchase where the engineer (when asked to give an estimate on the value) estimated the house to be worth $1.1 million to $1.2 million. The reality was that the buyer and seller had already agreed on a price of $325,000 and the surrounding homes were selling between $175,000 and $200,000. Market value on this particular house was probably close to $400,000 in its as-is condition. The moral of this story is that engineers and home inspectors are not generally qualified to give opinions on the value of properties.

Do Your Due Diligence—How to Get the Macro-View of Your Local Market

Before we get into establishing the value of your property, it is important to take the pulse of the surrounding market conditions and trends. Later in this book, we will discuss how you can utilize the services of an appraiser or real estate agent to help you gather data about the market in general. Getting the macro-view data is a bonus that you can ask of the appraiser or agent, since they often use this information anyway. Market trend information can also be obtained through the local Multiple Listing Service (MLS) or various online third-party resellers. However, when it comes to third-party information, make sure that the data is accurate, timely, and complete. If you are not going to hire a real estate agent on a full service basis (see Chapter 6), you may be able to get this information from a real estate agent who acts as a facilitator for a fraction of the traditional commission structure. Facilitators will be discussed in more detail in Chapter 6.

The Supply Quotient—An Extremely Valuable Number

The supply quotient is simply a ratio of the number of homes for sale in your area divided by the number of closings in the last 30 days. The supply quotient is a very useful indicator of supply and demand in your neighborhood. It helps you estimate the number of months it would take to sell your home if you do what most people do, without following the special techniques in this book.

To figure out the supply quotient, you first need to decide on the boundaries of your local market. This is called your "defined geography." It's the area where houses are similar to yours. A professional appraiser typically looks at houses in the same subdivision and so should you. But be careful with "dividing lines." Geographic dividing lines such as opposing sides of the river, the park, or a main highway can be invisible dividing lines that put the property in another school district and may not be within your defined geography.

Next, you need to ask a real estate agent to give you two pieces of data to make a ratio. The amount number of houses currently for sale in your defined geography will be the numerator in your ratio. This is the supply figure. The denominator is the number of houses that have sold in the last 30 days. "Sold" is defined as closed transactions; however, under contract or opened escrow transactions are sometimes used as a forward-looking gauge. Once you divide the number of homes for sale by the number of sales in the last 30 days, you have the supply quotient, or the number of months that it will take to sell all the homes within your defined geography at the rate that homes are currently selling. For example, if 60 houses are for sale and 10 have sold in the last month, then the supply quotient is 6. Thus, if no other houses went on the market, it would take six months to sell all the current inventory.

A supply quotient of six is a market in which sellers and buyers are balanced and equal in force. The lower the quotient, the better the market is for sellers, hence a sellers market. The greater the quotient is above six, the better the market is for buyers, which indicates a buyers market. Understanding this quotient and especially its trend over the last few months (moving up or down) has saved sellers tens of thousands of dollars and a great deal of time.

The supply quotient is to the seller what radar and sonar are to the captain of a ship. It's hard to imagine navigating the housing market without it. It gives you the macro-view of the market. If the supply quotient trend indicates a strengthening market, and you know this, then being prepared at the time of negotiations to say "no" is powerful stuff as long as you know whether the market conditions are on your side. Perhaps one the most important points that we can make here is also the converse. If the supply quotient trend indicates the market is softening, you know you're going to need to say "yes" quickly, even if you don't like the offer, and you'll have to make whatever concessions are necessary to get the deal done. If you don't know the supply quotient, and the market is softening you'll lose out one deal after another.

Knowing your macro (or supply quotient) conditions is the first step toward the right mindset when needing to get it sold within a particular time period. We refer to the supply quotient as the theoretical amount of time that it will take to sell all the homes on the market at the current rate of closed transactions. If you don't need to sell and enjoy playing the lottery, then price it as high as you like. However, if the quality of your life will be hurt by not selling (and your decision to get it done with is paramount), then don't play games with pricing.

Sometimes You Are a Winner When You Lose

Ralph had purchased a home with his wife right at the peak of the last market cycle in New York (1987). Ralph had some unexpected financial problems caused by the crash of the stock market, a divorce, and a job loss. At this point, he became a very motivated seller. He enlisted a top agent in the area, who also happened to a good friend. After studying the relative neighborhood sales, and calculating the supply quotient, it became apparent that they would need to price the house at less than the price Ralph had just paid for the home one year earlier. The supply quotient told them the market was changing rapidly. At the time, a 10 percent loss on the home seemed to be too much to bear for Ralph. But, because he had to sell and he trusted the agent's advice, Ralph agreed to take one of the first offers he had on the house, which was a loss of 10 percent. Four years later, the house was worth 30 percent less than Ralph had originally paid for the house. It was only then he considered himself to be lucky to have listened to his agent and to the supply quotient trend.

On Wall Street, many a trader has said, "Bulls make money and bears make money, but pigs get slaughtered." In real estate, pricing the property with an eye on the supply quotient and the greater market forces is key to avoiding the unrecoverable mistake of mispricing a house when it first goes on the market. Imagine a love story where the beautiful princess is being courted by the handsome prince. He tells her he wants to visit her. She tells him she has a long list of conditions and prerequisites that will take weeks of work for the prince to complete before she'll even consider a date. Meanwhile, the line of princesses is forming at the prince's front door. It's critical to know the supply of princesses and the available qualified princes is your area, before you make to many demands of your princes.

Watch Out for Seasonal Trends.   The home sales data in the last three months in your defined geography is the best indicator of the current condition of the market. However, you should also compare this information with sales during the same quarter of the prior year. You should also take into account the seasonal fluctuations of the market that can often create inconsistencies in pricing. For example, if you're selling in January and looking at properties sold from Thanksgiving through Christmas, it may appear the market is worse than it is because of the lower activity in number of sales. Likewise, in October you may be looking at the previous summer's robust sales and not taking into account the possibility that the months ahead may be slower.

The Micro-View of Your Local Market

The micro-view looks at the neighborhood level and how your home fits in. At this level we're going beyond the market factors in general and looking at particular values within your specific geographic area—the closer to your house, the better.

Comparable Sales

Appraisers typically use the following three ways to estimate a property's value:

- Comparable sales approach
- Replacement cost approach
- Income approach

The comparable sales method is the most commonly used— and thought to be the most accurate one—to determine the value of single-family homes, condominiums and smaller rental buildings (two to four units).

Start by researching information about sold properties on your local government web sites for your target area. Many tax assessor's offices and county courthouses offer searchable online databases that allow you to view the prices for properties within a specific area. They usually list full details about the properties, including square footage. Plus, subscriber web sites such as Electronic Appraiser (www.electronicappraiser.com) give you detailed information, particularly in areas where online data is scarce. Free web sites such as Zillow (www.zillow.com) also offer property data, but the information is less detailed than for the paid sites. For example, the seller's name may be missing, which could be relevant if the seller was a bank, as in the case of a foreclosure sale. If that's the case, it can't be considered a comparable sale because the property was sold in distress.

Be careful about using web sites that offer a computer-generated valuation. These are called automated valuation models (AVMs), which aggregate sales data from comparable properties to determine an estimated price. While AVMs can be a benchmark for determining value, they can be off by as much as 10 percent or more. With a little research, you can pinpoint the value to as close as 3 to 5 percent.

The most useful computer database for getting information about comparable properties is the local MLS. This database shows the number of days the house has been on the market and includes notes that indicate whether the property was updated, whether the seller offered concessions on the sale, and so on. This additional data is generally not available through other sources, so asking a real estate agent or appraiser to help you will be crucial, because most MLS systems aren't accessible to the general public.

While many factors come into play when you're evaluating a residential property's value by "comps" (comparable sales), the three key factors are location, size (square footage) of the home, and the number of bedrooms and bathrooms. Obviously, you'll need to look at many other aspects before you can pinpoint the exact value of a property, but these are the big three. You should be able to look at comparable sales involving properties with these three factors and get a good idea of the value of the property you're selling.

Location is extremely important when you're comparing sold properties. A professional appraiser typically looks at houses within a one-mile radius or less, and so should you. In the case of a subdivision—where the houses are all similar and built in the same time period—you need to compare similar houses with similar styles in the same subdivision to get an accurate valuation. If there's a wide mix of properties in the subdivision, you may need to go outside of it to get comparable sales. Just be careful with dividing lines. Geographic lines such as opposite sides of the river, the park, or a main highway can be invisible dividing lines that put the property in another school district and may not garner equitable comps.

When determining a home's value, be sure to evaluate the square footage. Note that appraisers typically look at homes that are within 20 percent up or down in square footage as comparables. Generally (especially within a subdivision), most homes fall within a fairly limited size range. Therefore, you should be able to develop a good gauge for the selling price of homes in those particular sizes.

Of course, not all square footage is created equal. Most people think that if a house has 1,000 square feet and is worth $100,000, then the 1,100 square-foot house next door would be worth $110,000. Wrong! The extra 10 percentage points in square footage equals only a few percentage points in value. If these two houses offer the same location, style, and number of bedrooms and baths, the 10 percent additional square footage won't change the valuation much. Why? Because there is a fixed cost on a house based on the value of the land, cost of construction, sewer, subdivision plans, and other factors. An extra few hundred feet of space involves very little cost—only wood, nails, carpet, and possibly some minor electrical and plumbing costs.

As we'll discuss later in this book, the number of bathrooms and bedrooms is more relevant than simply the raw square footage. In other words, a three-bedroom home with 1,200 square feet might be worth more than a two-bedroom home with 1,250 square feet. It also matters where the bedrooms and bathrooms are located—on the main floor or the basement. While finished basements can add value, the amount of that value is less than it is for above-ground living areas. Plus, this greatly varies depending on different regions of the country. In humid areas, below-ground living space isn't as valuable to homeowners as it is in dryer areas of the country.

To determine a home's value using comps, also look at the quality and number of bedrooms and bathrooms. Three-bedroom homes are generally a big plus over two-bedroom homes, but four or five-bedroom homes don't add as much over a three-bedroom if they are roughly the same size in square footage. Likewise, two bathrooms is a big plus over one bathroom, but three or more don't add as much value.

When comparing bathrooms, make sure you understand the different types of bathrooms and compare them correctly. A full bathroom includes a shower, bath, toilet and sink. A three-quarter bath has a shower but no tub, plus a toilet and sink. A half bath has a toilet and sink but no tub or shower. A three-quarter-bath creates roughly the same value as a full-bath, particularly if another bathroom in the house has a tub. A half-bath has less value unless there are enough other bathrooms in the house. Also, a five-piece bath (separate shower and tub) generally wouldn't add more value than a regular full bathroom with a combination shower and tub.

There are other factors to consider that affect the value of a home, but generally you'd give these less weight than the location, size, and number of bedrooms and bathrooms. Some houses have one-car or two-car garages, some have carports, and others have neither. The garage factors in some value, depending on the rest of the neighborhood. For example, if the neighborhood comps all have two-car garages, this can affect value as much as 10 percent on the subject property if it has only a one-car garage or no garage. However, if the houses are all small and there's a mix of garage options, the garage won't be as big of an issue. Likewise, a four-car garage in a three-car-garage-neighborhood probably won't count for much either. One exception is with condominium developments. Parking spots or garages are generally sold with condominiums and can have substantial value, particularly in large cities where parking is limited to the street.

In most cases, a swimming pool won't affect the value of a property. In most regions of the country, a pool may actually diminish the value because it's considered a safety issue and may take up precious space on the backyard. In hot regions like Arizona or southern Florida, though, a small dipping pool is a nice feature. However, it still won't add value in a significant way.

The Comp Book. You should develop your own comp book of data that's relevant and specific to your house and the immediate competition in terms of style, square footage, and location. You will want to stick with information about your defined geography, as we discussed earlier.

The comp book will be your best friend throughout the process, because it provides the factual data around which you will base not only your decisions, but also your advertising, marketing, and sales pitch. This will be core data that will be indisputable by any professional (agent, appraiser, home inspector, lender, or insurance agent) you may come across throughout the transaction.

The comp book should contain the following information:

- **Sold homes.** List homes closest to your own in terms of location, style, size, and utility. In other words, if you have a ranch, try to find other ranches. If you have a three-bedroom home, try to find other three-bedroom homes. For purposes of comparison, the houses on your own block are better than houses farther away, but anything in the same subdivision will generally suffice, so long as it is similar in size. The most recent sales are the most relevant, and while appraisers will generally consider sales six months old in a normal market, you should stick with the most recent (two to three months old) sales in a declining market. If you can't find such recent comps, then you can look at more recent sales of homes that are different in style and within a radius of up to one mile, assuming you don't go outside the neighborhood boundaries. You can go to surrounding neighborhoods so long as they are similar in schools, price ranges, size, style, and age of homes.

- **Under-contract homes.** Using the same guidelines as above, you want to know all of the relevant properties that are currently under contract. This will tell you where the market is currently heading in terms of current demand. Note the difference between the asking and selling prices of these homes, which can be obtained by calling the listing agent's office.

- **Homes for sale.** In a declining market, homes currently for sale are even more important than homes sold, for purposes of comparison because they will indicate the pricing trend. In fact, you should check for new homes listed for sale and current homes for sale price changes every week in your neighborhood to keep an eye on your competition.

- **Neighborhood information.** Gather all pertinent information about schools, zoning, homeowners associations, neighborhood amenities, local shopping, and attractions.

- **Expired listings.** Look at houses that were listed for sale and did not sell. The question you have to determine is "Why did it not sell." In most cases, the answer is that the property was mispriced. However, many times the problem was a lack of effective marketing. It is a good idea to determine which scenario occurred. The owner may have been uncooperative with the agent in showing the property or keeping the property in a presentable state. The agent may have either made an error or done a poor job in listing the property, limiting the full exposure to the marketplace. Since buyers use the computer to screen properties, poor or missing photos, wrong schools, the incorrect size of the house, wrong number of bedrooms, and other information can result in fewer buyers who are interested in viewing the property. Speaking to the owner and the listing agent will give you two of the three possible versions of the truth, the last of which is your job to determine!

- **Bracketing.** Bracketing is the idea of determining where your house is positioned within a group of competitors, whether sold, under contract, or for sale. For example, you would want to find a half dozen properties superior to yours and a half dozen inferior to yours within the criteria discussed above; then analyze the prices to determine where you fit.

- **The quantity of data.** Obviously, you don't want to over- or underanalyze the information in your market. We've found that a comprehensive amount of data at the micro-view level would be the best dozen sold, the best dozen under contract, the best dozen expired listings, and the best dozen houses for sale.

- **The quality of the data.** Bear in mind that all sales are not what they appear to be. Verification of the data is often done by picking up the phone and asking the agent if the sales price was the actual sales price or whether it included seller concessions such as monies for closing costs or repairs or other miscellaneous items. Occasionally, a sale price will make no sense and will be way out of line with what would seem to be a reasonable value. In these cases, simply disregard that data as an anomaly. Inter-family sales, foreclosure sales, and estate sales are some examples.

- **Timeliness of data.** The timeliness of this data must be considered in relation to the macro-view. In other words, if the market is changing as determined by the macro-view, then an appropriate time-value adjustment will be necessary at the end of our calculations. Lastly, the uniqueness and rarity of your type of property can have positive value implications, assuming that the buyers in the market will appreciate them. This adjustment is determined here and now at the micro-level. For example, assuming you do your research and estimate your property's worth at $250,000, and you also know that prices are declining 1 percent per month, you need to be able to price your property to keep ahead of this curve.

- **The defined area.** Appraisers and loan underwriters generally look at comparables sales within one mile of the subject property. However, in populated cities, one mile may be too far. In rural areas, one mile may be too close. Within a subdivision, you'll find variations in lots that affect privacy, road noise, or sunlight. These lot variations won't affect the valuation unless an extreme difference exists. For example, if a row of houses backs to a major road, this may drop the value of the house by as much as 10 percent. If a row of houses backs to power lines or a garbage dump, the discount may be even more substantial.

On the other hand, a great view may affect the lot substantially—in a positive way, of course. A location on a golf course, lake, ocean, or simply having a killer view may push values up by 25 percent.

What Is Assessed Value?

County tax assessors value property for tax purposes. This is called the assessed value. This figure usually has some bearing on market value, but don't rely on its real market value. Instead, look at the assessed value as it compares to sold prices on the comparable properties as a reference point.

In some parts of the country, assessed value is a formula based on real value so the amount is more reliable. In either event, use the assessed value only as a benchmark. For example, if the assessed value of homes in your farm area is generally 90 percent of market value and your subject property is listed for double the assessed value, something may be wrong!

Take note of the tax-assessed land value versus the improvements, then note what the average lot premium or discount amounts to. You can check the lot premium in new home developments by asking the builder. In more established areas, the home sale records of similar houses in the neighborhood will be reflected in the prices of houses sold that are the same model, but have different lots. Amateurs often make the mistake of comparing houses that are across the street from each other, overlooking the fact that the lots have significant variations.

Chapter Summary

- Knowledge is power—organize your information.
- Hire an inspector to root out any safety issues.
- Develop a comps book with data about the market.

CHAPTER 3

The Secret of Effectively Pricing Your House for a Quick Sale

Price is what you pay. Value is what you get.
—Warren Buffett

Once you've compiled the data and understand the macro- and micro-views of the market, you need to get out of your chair and into the street to get real-world street smarts. The most successful sellers of real estate find their best buyers out in the field while they're checking out the competition and determining where to price their property and how to dress it up to out-value the competitors. Most importantly, you'll need to gain knowledge of the market that you can draw upon in conversation with confidence when the inevitable negotiations start. Remember that buyers want to get your property for the lowest possible price. Assuming they recognize your property as the best value on the market, it now becomes a matter of convincing them the value is there, and your persuasiveness is based on your ability to share that information with them quickly and at the right time.

All successful agents know that it's not just what you say, but how you say it that gets buyers to up their offer to the highest possible amount. The ability to access the sales data at the tip of your tongue will give you and the buyer a place of factual reference based on the realities of the market, instead of the often erroneous and negative information spewed out by the media.

Know Thy Competition

It's time to play *I-Spy* and start looking at the supply on the market, that is, your competition. There's no substitute for driving around the neighborhoods and getting a real assessment of what's out there in the market.

The Drive-By

As you drive by the properties, it's important to keep track of what you see and what you think of the value of that property. It's often inconvenient to gain entry to houses that have sold, yet the ones for sale can be viewed by simply calling the agent or the seller in the case of a for-sale-by-owner (FSBO) property. We recommend that you first view all properties from the outside, giving each a name that will help you remember them after you've viewed all of your comps. For example, most of the comps will have a picture that will help; however, locations of these properties need to be adjusted for and noted if the location is exceptionally good or bad. These cases often are the most miscalculated, since location can have the greatest affect on values. A cul-de-sac location versus a main street location can have a 20 percent value swing (10 percent more or less) especially if the main street location has additional negative factors such as being downstream from a gas station or next to a water or electrical tower.

Rating the Comps on Value Not Condition

Every comp you view needs a rating. This rating should be on a scale of one to five with five being the best value for the money. A mansion for a low price would be a five. The same mansion for twice what it's worth is a one. A handyman for a giveaway price would be a five. Ratings are based on relative value based on the asking and sold prices, as they may be. The point of this is to ultimately determine what price it would take to make your property a five compared to the houses currently for sale and the ones that have sold already.

This rating process will give you the edge over almost all of the competition because rarely do even the professionals take the time to do this for each property. But the best gift we can give you is the gift of knowledge and preparation before putting your house up for sale and before renovating or staging the house. This way, your efforts are market driven, because valuation has been determined by the market, not fantasy.

We once worked an area where Caribbean buyers were paying huge premiums for houses that reminded them of home. It was the informed sellers and professionals who recognized the trend in their comp books that gave them the advantage. Specifically it wasn't much more than the striking colors of their home town that made a significant difference to them. Even though the key feature was just paint; it was amazing how they reacted to what we know as one of the three most effective things sellers can do to their property in preparation for selling. As we'll discuss in more detail in Chapter 4, landscaping, carpeting, and painting are almost always the best bang for the buck.

What's Hot and What's Not

Today's closest competitors to your property will need the closest monitoring and inspection for value. Since these houses will be viewed by your buyer as a possibility for home ownership, it's here that success lives and dies. Imagine you were no longer a seller, but a buyer. As objectively as possible, try to keep in mind that what sellers are now asking is not necessarily what the house is worth. In fact it's just a price point that you're using to compare the overall competition first and to get a lineup of properties that are valued as fives. You will then find ways to price your property into that category. Otherwise, your biggest expense will be the time wasted and aggravation caused by chasing a declining market.

Pricing *Your* House: The No-Brainer and Giggle Tests

Now that you're armed with information about comparable sales, it's time to determine a price.

Paradox of Pricing

Most people think pricing their property as high as possible to begin with will yield the highest final price. This may be furthest thing from the truth. The price at which you initially offer your house for sale is one of the most important factors in getting it sold quickly. Having the wrong price is the primary mistake sellers make in any market.

So, what price should you offer for the property's value? The obvious answer is to drop the price so low that people will be swarming in with interest, when you first put it up for sale. This is a mistake for two reasons. First, people could think there's something wrong with the house if you list too low. There's a psychological effect to a product or service being priced too low, which is why most products and services have a price range. Take, for example, a television set. If you walk into Best Buy and look at a 48-inch LCD screen, you'll notice that most brands are priced in the same ballpark. There's also some Korean brand you've never heard of priced well below the rest. It looks the same and smells the same, but something in your gut tells you it can't be as good. The same psychology often applies to houses—don't price it too low, or you'll spook away some of the buyers.

On the other hand, pricing a property deliberately low can have the opposite effect, that is, to invite people to overbid on the listing. Some sellers actually use an auction method with a low reserve bid to get a frenzy going, a technique we'll discuss in Chapter 10.

The second and more important reason you don't want to price the property too low is that you're leaving money on the table. Obviously, there's a balance you need to strike between your natural desire to get the most money and your practical, sensible side that tells you to price it to move quickly. The important thing is to price it *right*, not to price it cheap. There are other factors that motivate people to sell, as we'll discuss later in this chapter, so don't fall into the trap of thinking that dropping the price is the only way to get it sold quickly. Price is only *one* factor of many for your buyers.

Another prime mistake is to price a property too high at first, with the thought that you can always drop the price. Some agents will quote you a high value in order to convince you to list the property with them. The property is listed at an unrealistically high price, and then the price must be dropped to face the reality of the market.

If the property sits on the market too long with a series of price drops, this can hurt you in one of two ways. It can show you're too eager, leading to lowball offers. Secondly, it could result in buyers wondering, *What's wrong with this house?* This will scare away buyers. As with a house priced too low, buyers will inevitably think to themselves, *Why has this property been sitting on the market so long? What am I missing?*

Months and months go by, and the house still won't sell, requiring the price to be dropped even more. Had you listed it at the right price from the outset, it would have sold at a better price than your final price-drop, which resulted from pricing it too highly to begin with. Your property will inevitably become stale from being on the market too long. If you have already done this, we recommend the "rebake" strategy discussed in Chapter 6.

Don't Push Your Luck

Ron tried to sell his house at the top of the market where, at the time, prices in his neighborhood ranged from $550,000 to $600,000. Ron tried to test the limits of his neighborhood by asking $625,000, figuring he could drop the price if he got no offers. Ultimately, it took a year to sell his house, with a final price of $535,000. Had he initially priced it at $575,000, it would have likely sold at close to his asking price and within a few months.

The Price-Range Listing

An effective strategy used in many markets across the country is to price the listing as a range rather than a set price. The price range is a bracketed price within 5 percent above and 5 percent below the actual target price. The idea behind this is to offer two things: first, the ability to lure lower-priced buyers to your price point, thereby increasing demand for your property. Who hasn't ever spent *slightly* more than the originally intended price, when recognizing value? Using the comp book to nudge buyers higher than they originally wanted to go can be done very effectively by proving the higher value as you share the acquired information you have developed, before you put the property on the market.

Secondly, the price-range listing provides the successful buyer with the ever popular bragging rights to friends and family.

Especially in a declining market, buyers will need to justify how great a deal they really got and how much money they saved from the asking price, which they may tend to think of and quote as the highest part of the range listing. How the price-range listing is negotiated will be discussed in Chapter 9.

Here's a good place to incorporate two strategies that we've talked about in regard to the most effective price for your property. Now that you've completed your due diligence, you probably have a very good idea of an approximate range of values that your property will fall within. This is what we consider to be the price range you will list your property at, if you can do so. The boundaries of this price-listing concept can be viewed as what we call the giggle and the no-brainer tests. The no-brainer test is the lower boundary at which you are sure that almost any reasonable buyer ("ready, willing, and able," in realty parlance) would pay for this property. The higher boundary is the giggle, that is, the place at which even you might think is overpriced. Find the middle point of those two boundaries, and let's call that the sweet spot. Now add and subtract 5 percent up and down to get the general price range. Notice that your giggle boundary and your no-brainer boundaries are greater than your general price-range differential.

Fine Tuning Your Price Range: Be the Best in Your Class.
The last step is to fine-tune the general price range to the ultimate and most effective price range. From your comp book, you'll find that many homes fall into general price categories or groupings. We'll continue to refer to these as "price classes." For example, in the $200,000 to $300,000 price range, there are four price classes— from $200,000 to $225,000, $225000 to $250,000, $250,000 to $275,000, and $275,000 to $300,000. So, if you have a house valued at $240,000, you would be better to price your property between $225,000 and $249,000, because many buyers tend to look within their budget range, which many times falls within psychological price ranges. You'll notice your local market's price classes from the comp book. You may notice that the price classes of houses that have been sold all tend to be within a particular range much more frequently than the availability of price classes in the for-sale category. To simplify the process, determine the number of houses for sale most similar to your house and what price range they tend to fall within. Then try to price your home most effectively

against the competition. It's better to ask less and be less flexible, because of the greater exposure you will give your property at the lower price.

The Psychology of Pricing

Retail experts warn against pricing items in round numbers. For example, stores rarely sell items for $10. Instead, they mark them at $9.99, sacrificing a penny on every sale. On the conscious level, we don't care about the one-cent discount, when we buy a DVD for $9.99 instead of $10, but on a subconscious level, studies show we are much more likely to buy an item priced at $9.99 than one at $10. You can apply the same logic by pricing your home at $249,000 instead of $250,000, or $799,000 instead of $800,000.

Always try to beat the competition by a degree, keeping in mind the psychology of the numbers. Let's say hypothetically there are 10 houses listed for $299,000. Your house should be listed for $297,000. Let's say there are 10 houses listed between $290,000 and $299,000. Your property should be listed at $289,000.

Ending in eight is not worth the while, because if you can get $298,000, you can get $299,000. On the other hand, seven is a lucky number ($297,000). One of the most misleading and annoying aspect of pricing is overdoing the numbers, such as $298,999. Such exact pricing suggests inflexibility and discourages offers.

You're Only as Good as Your Information

Since your house is one of your most valuable assets (and most significant liabilities); you should verify the data. Hire an appraiser and/or a real estate agent to assist you in compiling the information, but ultimately trust your own opinions and ideas to determine what your property is worth—and what it can be worth with minor modifications and improvements. This can only be determined once you've done your homework and looked at the property through the eyes of the buyer as objectively as possible.

The Appraisal Trap.   Don't be fooled by an appraisal. An appraisal is a certification by a licensed professional that a house is worth a certain amount based on comparable sales. It's an opinion of value based on one person's analysis and experience. The actual market value is the amount a buyer is willing to pay and a seller is willing to sell under normal circumstances.

The appraiser drives his opinion by looking through the rearview mirror. His analysis is predominately based on what has sold, not on what people will pay in the future. The economic trends are often not factored in until after the fact.

Another type of opinion of value is that of a real estate professional known as a broker's price opinion (or BPO). This type of market analysis shows properties that have sold, as well as properties for sale. In a declining market, that can be more accurate than an appraisal, so long as the agent is actively listing and selling properties like yours within the neighborhood.

Given a choice between an appraisal and a BPO, we would more highly value the BPO provided we were getting the *absolute truth* by the agent without any self-serving agendas of his own. In Chapter 6, we will reveal an unorthodox, but effective strategy for getting the truth from the agent without any bias or conflict of interest. In all fairness to agents, many feel compelled to give the best case scenarios of value in order to win over the business of the seller as a potential client. We all know that people will hear what they want to hear. As we have discussed, mispricing the property is the most costly mistake we can make.

Anticipating and Monitoring Change

Based on the macro-view, the market may or may not move in your favor. Being sensitive to the rate of change of the supply quotient will help you in determining how aggressively you should be pricing the property. For example, if the supply quotient is a double-digit number, and you need to sell your house quickly, you may need to significantly price your property ahead of the competition. This is where relative thinking in terms of percentages will save your neck. A $1,000 discount on a $10,000 car is a substantial amount because it represents about 10 percent. A 5 percent price advantage over the competition in real estate would be significant enough to create the demand to achieve the highest possible price while still maintaining the least amount of flexibility from your asking price.

Remember, it's a numbers game; you'll still have people low-balling you no matter what price you ask. The advantage of the right marketing price is that you should have between one and three bidders competing for your property in *any* market. At that point, it will be a matter of proper negotiating skills, in order to up the buyers' bidding to the highest possible price, instead of the giveaway price to one bidder when your starting offer was too high. In our experience, this has proven to be the most successful strategy pricewise and timing-wise that a seller can use, especially in a soft real estate market. Take it from us—we have handled more than 2,000 transactions over more than two decades—and we've made every mistake you can imagine. By virtue of experience we have figured out strategies that are counterintuitive, hard to swallow, but ultimately the best possible medicine to cure the ills within a sick real estate market.

Chapter Summary

- Picking a price point involves knowing your competition.
- Consider offering a price range instead of a fixed price.
- Price your house competitively below the competition.

CHAPTER 4

Preparing to Show Your House for Sale—You Only Get One Chance to Make a Good First Impression

Between two products equal in price, function and quality, the better looking will out sell the other.

—Raymond Loewy

Whether you're selling your principal residence or a fixer upper, you should have a sparkling, clean property to sell before you put it on the market. You must ensure that your property stands out from other listings if you want it to sell quickly. It must make a strong, positive impression. The good news is that you don't have to spend a fortune to get it to pop.

Deciding What to Renovate

Before putting your home on the market, you need to decide how much you're going to spend on time and labor in getting it ready for market. Before doing so, you need to look at the other houses in your area and do some homework. If you're asking the same price as your competition, which has a completely renovated kitchen, you'd better make sure your kitchen is also updated. If you decide not to renovate the kitchen, then you'll either have to drop the price or have some other selling features that justify the comparable price you're asking for your house.

Is Rehabbing for You?

Before you enter into an elaborate rehab, you must decide if it's for you. Some people like a hands-on approach. Other people are all thumbs and have no business doing fix-up work. Determine whether getting involved in a rehab is the most effective use of your time. If you have the money and can hire a contractor to handle your projects, then by all means do so. You can't afford to fall behind your schedule, or to go over budget.

Different Levels of Renovation

There are basically three levels of renovation in getting a house ready for market:

- Level 3: Complete Update
- Level 2: Cosmetic Update
- Level 1: Cosmetic Staging

Complete Update

A complete update means spending about 10 percent of the home's resale value on updating the kitchens and bathrooms. In places where the median home costs $500,000 for a 1,500-square-foot ranch, this is good news, because you will get your money's worth. In places where the same house sells for $125,000, it's bad news because the same house won't yield as much profit. The bottom line is that you should resist spending too much money because you will not likely reap the rewards. You'll want to spend only enough to get it sold at the price that makes sense, considering the time and money you spend on rehabbing it.

Both newbie and seasoned rehabbers habitually underestimate the time and expense needed to complete a renovation. Always estimate repairs conservatively, planning for the worst case scenario. Start with the outside, and work through the interior, room by room, step by step. Use the checklist in Appendix B of this book to come up with an estimate of repairs, and then add at least a 10 percent margin for error. If you sell the property for a good price, any overestimate will become an extra bonus.

If you never so much as picked up a hammer, a checklist means nothing. One way you will become better at estimating costs is to learn how the work is done. We're not suggesting that you learn the physical skills necessary to do each job, but rather the overall process. Once you understand the mechanics of each part of the job, you will become confident estimating repairs and negotiating with contractors. The major home improvement chains, such as Home Depot offer free classes everyday on everything from tiling kitchens to replacing windows. Books and videos on basic home improvement are also available from Home Depot, *Reader's Digest*, and Time-Life Books. Gathering this information will give you a good idea of the time, materials, and cost of the needed repairs.

Cosmetic Update

A cosmetic update is generally paint, carpet, and a few choice items that give it appeal. Your budget will depend on the size of your house, but generally $2,000 to $3,000 should be enough. Television shows on the HGTV cable channel such as *Sell This House* are good to watch for ideas. While the $2,000 budget on the show is a bit unrealistic considering labor costs, it does help you focus on the most important aspects of creating the necessary appeal for the least amount of money.

Paint and carpet go a long way toward sprucing up a dated home. Stick with colors that are warm, but neutral. White and off-white are dull and boring. Soft yellow, green, and blue can be used with an offsetting white trim. If you have dark-colored doors and trim, consider sanding and painting them a bright white using a semigloss paint. If you have nice, wood doors that are faded, a professional can glaze them darker for about $100 per door. If the doors are cheap or cracked, consider replacing them with hollow-core six- or eight-panel doors. Brass or pewter door knobs give a nice upgrade, too.

Overspend on the small items that are not expensive in the entire scope of things. For example, if you only need three light fixtures in the house, consider spending $100 rather than $25 on each one. If you have two bathrooms, a $50 faucet will make a bigger impact than a $10 faucet, but will only change your total budget by $80.

Avoid overspending on items that don't produce appeal. While quality products will appeal to the logic of the buyer, it will not persuade him to buy as much as things that create emotional appeal.

High-grade roofing, furnaces, and hot water heaters don't make the house look nicer. In fact, you should not replace any of these items unless they're completely shot and won't pass a safety inspection. If you replace the carpet, don't bother with an expensive stain-resistant product that costs extra, since this isn't something noticeable to the prospective buyers.

Cosmetic Staging

Cosmetic staging is necessary whether you update your property or not. We want to introduce you to a relatively new concept called "staging." Staging has been around for some time now, but with people having difficulty selling their homes in the present down market it has really begun to take on a whole new sense of urgency and importance. When the market was booming and houses were selling no matter what they looked like, staging was not as critical as it is today. In our opinion, this is going to be the single most important thing you can and will do to get your home sold quickly and for more money.

Staging is basically showmanship. Look at the Rolling Stones or Madonna. They don't just sing. Everybody sings. They have great stage presence, and they put on a show. People pay big money for a ticket to one of their concerts because they want to see the show. So staging is basically doing all the things that are necessary for your house to out-show your competition. Your house has to be the Madonna house of those around you, and people will pay more for it. If you do a great job of staging your home, you don't have to be a salesperson; you're a showman, and your house will sell itself.

You need to create some appeal to make your house stand out from the rest of the properties in the neighborhood. If you have ever visited a builder's model home, you've undoubtedly seen staging at work. Since people have very little imagination, a staged home helps people imagine what their things would look like if they moved into the home, even if their furnishings look completely different.

A Checklist of Staging Ideas

The following is a good checklist of things you can do to create more appeal to sell your home, whether it is renovated or not. You may not choose all of these things, but consider each of them as a checklist in preparing a plan to get your home ready for market.

Start with Curb Appeal

Walk all the way around the property and make sure there are no visible trashcans, recycling totes, garden hoses, or other eyesores. Don't ignore anything that takes away from your property's like-new appearance. Look for additional ways to create curb appeal. You can add flowerpots, hanging baskets, or perhaps a wreath or pine boughs during the winter months. Don't think you have to have a green thumb; quality faux plants look as good as real ones, and you can use them when the weather will not support live plants.

Remove window screens, then scrape and clean windows, sills, and knock down any spider webs. Look for and replace any cracked or fogged windows. If you don't replace them, the property inspector will point them out later. You can leave some or all of the screens off, and store them elsewhere on the grounds, to improve the home's views. Sweep the roof, and clean the gutters. While on the roof, look for torn shingles, or other things that need attention. Paint, tuck, point, caulk, or replace any weathered penetrations such as flues, chimneys, or roof vents.

Water the lawn, remove any weeds, mow, edge, and apply Revive or a similar product if you're in the summer months and the lawn is not in peak condition. Take off dead blooms, prune shrubs and trees, and add new colored mulch or pine straw to create a fresh appearance. Weed-blocking cloth is useful for landscaping, but make sure it's completely hidden by the appropriate ground cover.

Make sure the house is an inviting place to enter. The walkway to the front door should be well lighted. If there's a dark or potentially unsafe approach to the front door, you should add low-voltage lighting. It does not have to be elaborate or expensive. Just place four to six solar-powered lights along the walkway, so visitors can see where they are going (and, since solar-powered lights are removable, you can take them with you for the next property). Make sure the doorbell ringer is lighted, and that it has a pleasant tone. Many buyers like to ring the doorbell before entering. So don't let them start their tour by finding a broken doorbell. Check all doors to see if they work properly. Buyers will not tolerate squeaks, large gaps, sticking, or difficult-to-use keys. Make sure there are nice doormats at each entrance. These mats welcome visitors and will help protect carpets. Now it's time to prepare the inside of your home.

The Interior

Builders spend thousands of dollars on interior decorators and expensive furnishings for their model homes because they know what sells properties—emotion. You don't necessarily need to furnish the entire house with brand new, high-quality furnishings, but you can add a touch here and there. The idea is to create attraction, so a buyer falls in love with your house, not uses logic to make the decision.

Make Sure Everything Is Clean.   Start by making sure every inch of the house is as clean as possible. Wipe all woodwork and cabinetry with oil or rejuvenating cleaner. Polish or seal hardwood floors if needed. Remove all the dust from vents, ceiling fans, cabinets, and horizontal surfaces. If there's any doubt about the carpets, have them professionally cleaned. If the carpet is new, make sure all the loose pieces are vacuumed up and removed. If there's a fireplace, have it cleaned by a chimney sweep. You can even stick a few logs or an electric fire log in there for effect.

If you haven't done so already, replace the thermostat with a basic, programmable model. Discard and replace anything that looks used, such as sink strainers, ice-cube trays, fireplace grates and range drip pans. Replace only the things that would be noticed as missing. Walk through the house at a quiet time and listen for squeaks in doors, creaky floors, or any other sounds that can be eliminated. Make sure every light bulb in the house is working and every toilet-paper and paper-towel holder is filled.

Declutter the House.   If you're still living in the home, start by decluttering the house of at least one third of your personal furnishings. You should rent a storage unit and clear out a lot of the items in your kitchen cabinets, closets, and garage to make it look more spacious. Remove any extra end tables, sofas, chairs, or personal collections of crystal unicorns in your living room display case.

Rearrange the furniture so that there's a nice flow between rooms, removing anything that's awkward or blocks your path. Any loose electronic wires, CD/DVD racks, or other messy collections should also be removed. Any paperwork, clothing, exercise equipment, toys, or other loose items should be moved out or placed in bins so they're out of sight. You want to give the appearance that your house is spacious and free from clutter. A messy or cluttered house will look small and disorganized, turning off most of your potential buyers. Remember, their current home is probably too small and cluttered, too; they won't want to move into the same environment!

"Small Rooms Look Bigger with Less Stuff"

Bill employed this technique in a market where the average price was $325,000 and the average time on market for similar houses was 110 days. He sold his house in 43 days for $345,000. The reason? Small rooms and a small garage that looked bigger than his competition because most of the furniture and personal items were removed.

Adding Decorations. As with paint, decorations should remain relatively neutral, though you can add some color and texture when possible. Wall hangings, attractive curtains, and certain paints can be neutral, yet add personality to a home. Try to maintain a decorating style that complements the architecture and the age of the home. A warm, yet understated look lends a comfortable feeling to a home.

Vases, bowls with potpourri and candlesticks are just a few ideas. Dried flowers and pinecones, along with other items found in nature can be placed almost anywhere. Go to thrift stores, garage sales, and discount chains (such as Marshalls or Ross) that carry discontinued or slightly damaged items. Start collecting a set of nice colorful towels, soap dishes, chairs, side tables, faux plants, pictures, and other accent items that you can use in your next house.

The Foyer. The first impression is the most important. If the foyer is dull, add some accent rugs and a small table. The table should have a nice Plexiglas holder with an information flyer about the property and a place for real estate agents to leave their cards.

Furnishings. There's no need to furnish a house with bedroom furniture or other large pieces. For higher-end homes, you can rent complete bedroom sets, but sometimes an air mattress on four milk crates with nice linens will do the trick. Small or odd-shaped spaces can provide decorating challenges, and often leave buyers with a negative impression. If your property has such areas, make an extra effort to furnish them in a way that shows there is a solution. A dining room table complete with chairs, placemats, and a nice setting creates a homey atmosphere. If it fits the dining room very well, you can even negotiate the sale of the house by including these items.

Floors. In homes with floor coverings other than carpeting, use throw rugs in all rooms. With beautiful hardwood floors, the rugs should be used as accents, while larger rugs should hide unattractive floors.

Lighting. If there are no overhead lights in one or more of the bedrooms or the living room, try adding a few floor lamps. Keep key lights on at all times, and make it clear to those seeing the house that these lights are to remain on. In fact, you can make a house look a whole lot nicer simply by experimenting with differing varieties of light bulbs in the right places.

Plants. Small plant stands will add appeal and keep the plants off the floor. You can purchase standing ficus or palm trees and place them in fancy pots. Dried flowers are easier to deal with, and faux dried flowers are even easier! Craft-store chains such as Michaels have a virtually unlimited supply of these items.

Wallpaper. Wallpaper that is well-hung and has good seams can be painted over. Use a good primer, and paint it accordingly. If the paper is very dark, you may have trouble because it will take several coats of paint to cover it. Peel and sand out any rough spots before you prime.

If you have a border along the ceiling, you may have to remove the paper and sand it before painting. You can spray texture over wallpaper before painting by using a good oil-based primer, but only with quality wallpaper that's well-hung.

The Kitchen. The kitchen is the heart of the home, so it should look lived in. The kitchen should have a set of dishtowels, paper towels, and maybe some glass jars with colorful contents on the counters. Selected windows can show off tinted glass vases or sun catchers to add warmth. Make sure the oven, fridge, and stove are clean. An ugly fridge can really detract from the kitchen, so consider replacing the fridge or throwing it out. If your stove burners are ancient, cover them with decorative metal covers. A couple of well-placed hand towels will add color and cover up scratches in the appliances.

A message board with little notes on it makes a nice touch, as well as magnets on the fridge with shopping lists and kids' drawings (have your own kids draw them for an authentic look!). If your house is vacant, place small decorative settings throughout the kitchen countertop, such as

- Coffee maker, mug, and a bag of beans
- Wine bottle and two glasses
- Plates, silverware, napkins, and candles

These settings will give a nice, warm look to the home without having to go overboard decorating the entire house with furniture.

Bathrooms.   The bathrooms should also have matching towels, soap and tissue dispensers, and a candle or plug-in air freshener with a pleasant scent. A bathroom should have an attractive shower curtain, but pull it aside to reveal nice tile work. For just a few bucks more, a colored shower curtain and decorative curtain rings look great. A nice floor mat and a magazine rack give it a lived-in feel. Avoid the fuzzy toilet cover and matching rug. Replace old, wooden seats with new ones. If your toilet is dated or cracked, replace it with a new one. A tub that's been scratched or painted a harsh color can be resurfaced for a fraction of the cost of a new one. Make sure the mildew is removed from the tile and around the shower and tub. If necessary, recaulk the trim around the tub and shower.

If your bathroom is cluttered with soaps, shampoos, and cosmetics, make sure you clear them out before showing the home. If the home is vacant, add just a few items to make it look warm and inviting, such as candles in a master bath and rubber ducks in a kids bathroom. A colorful throw rug on the floor will add color and distract from any old-style tiles that may need replacing but aren't within your budget. If you're going to invest any money in bathrooms, focus on the master bathroom first, since this is the most important bathroom in the house.

A worn out vanity in a bathroom can be an eyesore. Remove an old medicine cabinet, and replace it with a decorative mirror. Instead of replacing an old wooden cabinet, simply spray on a coat of semi-gloss white paint and replace the hardware with more modern pieces. If your cabinet is loaded up with hairspray, shampoo, and cosmetics, place them neatly in plastic bins so that it looks more organized.

Wall Hangings.   Place a few pictures, wall hangings, and a mirror or two throughout the house, one item in each bedroom and at least two in the kitchen and family rooms. Hang the pictures on the walls, at or below eye level, or simply lean them against the walls at floor level. Don't use cheap-looking artwork. You can buy used artwork at garage sales or scratch and dent items at discount stores like Ross or TJ Maxx.

Window Coverings.   Window shades give character to any house, but don't block a good view or sunlight. Use them in the rooms that may have especially bad views, including finished basements. Pleated shades block marginal views while letting light into a room, whereas mini-blinds provide a cleaner look without hiding what's outside. Home improvement centers carry inexpensive blinds that can be custom-sized while you wait. Blinds with larger two-inch faux-wood slats are affordable and especially nice. Tilt the blinds down so that buyers can see the yard if there's a good view. For basement windows, you can even use the temporary paper shades to camouflage an ugly window well.

If you have a nice yard or view, or want to get the maximum exposure of light, skip the shades entirely and use a decorative curtain rod and sheer curtains. Stick with white, beige, or another soft color that complements the color scheme in the room.

Working the Senses.   Do not underestimate the power of smell! It's true that scents leave a lasting impression on people. You want potential buyers to associate a pleasant fragrance with your property, even if that association is on a subconscious level. Start by neutralizing any existing unpleasant or musty smells created by mildew, garbage, or lack of fresh air. If you've done any rehab work, there will be lingering fumes including new paint, carpet, adhesive, or floor sealants, even though the house is immaculate.

If possible, open all windows during the final few days of preparation, and keep air moving through the house. If necessary, bring in portable fans to help circulate fresh air. Sprinkle baking soda through the house, leave it for several days, and vacuum the floors using a clean bag. Utilize natural cleaning products such as vinegar and citrus oil in this last stage to avoid a hospital-like smell. Lastly, use natural air fresheners such as fresh-cut flowers, pine boughs, or quality potpourri. The plug-in air fresheners work well, too, particularly in bathrooms.

Consider playing some soothing music in the house for your showings. New Age, soft jazz, or classical can create different ambiences. You can even have different music playing in different parts of the home to create a different environment—fun music in the kitchen, soft music in the bedroom.

Unfinished Areas. Don't forget to inspect the basement or crawlspace, attic or other unfinished areas. Add lighting to these areas. Even battery-powered lights will be much better than nothing. Make sure they are completely clean. It's surprising how many listings have construction debris and other unsightly things lying around. If there's an ugly window well in the basement, clean it out and paint it a neutral color.

It's fairly common to see what appears to be a well-prepared listing, and then, upon visiting these unfinished areas, make unpleasant discoveries. A few examples include sewer-line debris, mousetraps, animal remains, furnace filters and ducts full of construction debris, building materials, cigarette butts, and drawers full of sawdust. Your goal is to show every space in the best possible way. The only evidence of renovations should be well-marked cans of paint, spare shingles, and similar items in an appropriate place. It's also worthwhile to have an area to display product warranty information, a sprinkler system map, and winterizing instructions. These items would typically be on a table or counter, along with other information regarding the property, loan options, home-owners' association information and other positive information about the neighborhood.

Make It Unforgettable

Keep in mind that people have been driving around your neighborhood or subdivision and looking at anywhere from 5 to 40 homes, so you better make sure your home makes a great and lasting first impression. You must keep in mind that a typical couple has been driving around all weekend looking at homes for sale, and if they've been looking at typical ranch-style three-bedroom, two-bath, two-car attached garage homes, how are they going to remember one house from another? More important, how are they going to remember your home? If they look at only three or four homes they may be able to remember, but after three or four they all start to look alike, and they can't just say to one another, "Remember honey, the three-bedroom, two-bath house we looked at"? Thus, you as the home seller must do something special that will make your home not only appealing, but *unforgettable*.

You don't have to necessarily spend a lot of money to make your house unforgettable. For example, a bright orange living room is unforgettable—not necessarily in a good way—but when the buyers are discussing the houses they visited, they won't forget the house with the orange living room. Although the general consensus is that you shouldn't use strong colors or too many personal decorations in a house, a few small, memorable touches will spark the emotions of your buyers and create a memorable experience for them. We call these emotional anchors.

Here are a few examples of emotional anchors:

- Place some old board games in the kids' playroom or basement
- Leave some seasoning decorations in plain view, such as Halloween candy and pumpkins in October, American flags in July, or poinsettias in December
- Hang a prom dress in one of the children's rooms
- Have an open chest with a wedding album and wedding dress in the attic

Emotional anchors create a memorable experience that reminds people of a happy time in their life. This will make them more likely to remember your house. Emotional anchors are inexpensive, fun, and creative, so use them as much as you can throughout your house.

Additional Tidbits

Each room should be equipped with a light-sensing, night light so that potential buyers can find their way around. Remember that many showings take place after dark, so the house should seem safe and should be easy to see at any time of day. If there's a hallway or other space with a missing light switch, a wall-mounted remote-control switch is a simple fix. These little improvements can make the difference between your property selling and not selling. You can place small handwritten signs through the house to point out various features. These notes will have the effect of a guided tour and will highlight selling points that may otherwise go unnoticed. Examples of things to point out would be dimmer switches, a special thermostat, appliance features, wiring upgrades, cable or computer outlets, architectural highlights, or anything new.

Assess the property to see where it falls short of current building codes. At a minimum, provide new smoke detectors, grounded receptacles, and ground-fault-circuit interrupters throughout. Most starter homes are purchased by families with children, so it pays to identify and remove potential hazards. Examples include railings with wide spacing between slats, sharp edges, windows exposed to large drop-offs, easy access to unfinished or dangerous areas outside. You can't eliminate all hazards, but you can make improvements such as adding latches or locking handsets, sanding sharp edges, and adding strategic buffers such as furniture.

Engage the Help of Others

The idea is to upgrade the appearance of the property, so don't use cheap-looking items or ones that seem too personal in taste. You may feel qualified to make all the decisions regarding your décor and presentation, but it would be wise to get second opinions from interior decorators, friends, or real estate experts. Visit show homes in new neighborhoods to gather ideas. You can even borrow a few items from your friends or relatives if there's not too much sentimental attachment.

There are professional companies that will decorate the entire house and bring the furniture with them. Depending on the size of the house and price range, this may make sense. It's not uncommon for sellers to pay upwards of $10,000 to professionally decorate a

$1 million home. We feel this may be overkill in a small starter home or condominium under $250,000. Although the term "Home Staging" is trademarked, it has become a common expression in the industry that refers to the process of decorating a house for resale.

Last, remember that properties being shown require continued cleaning to look presentable. Properties that have been renovated will continue to show residual dust left from sanding floors and dry-wall. Some listings have signs asking people to remove their shoes. While this practice in essence points out clean or new carpets, it doesn't invite potential buyers to make themselves at home. Build-ers showcasing immaculate homes don't ask such things of buyers, and it is not recommended in this book.

Fortunately, most people respect other people's property, espe-cially when accompanied by their real estate agent. Still, it's amaz-ing how much of a mess inconsiderate people can make when showing properties. They sometimes track in dirt, leave their trash behind, leave water running and don't flush toilets after using them. A recent listing that was vacant had major water damage because someone left a window open during a tour. When the temperature dropped later that night, a pipe burst and damaged the bathroom and hardwood floors. In addition to the cost of repairs, several potential buyers were left with a bad impression, and the property had to be taken off the market while repairs were completed. Visit the property often to clean floors, dust, tend to lawns, and check for any other problems.

Hiring a Staging Professional

If you feel you won't be up to the task, you might consider hiring a staging professional. There are various levels of staging, from all-out furniture rental to small, decorative arrangements. Interview several people to get a feel for how you can work with someone. A good place to start is the real estate services directory of your local paper or try Google (for instance, "home staging Fresno, CA").

Consider the following questions when hiring a professional home stager:

- Do I feel comfortable working with this person?
- Does this person seem to understand my needs?
- Does she appear confident with my project?

- Is she upfront with her fees?
- Does she have the time to devote to my project?

Make sure that your staging professional has experience in selling homes that are similar in location, price range, and style to your home. Ask for references and a portfolio of pictures. See if there are any existing homes she has staged that you can look at.

How to Finance Your Renovations

If you have the cash, financing your renovations is not a big issue; the real issue is whether you're willing to put up the money to get the house sold. From an emotional standpoint, some homeowners feel that they don't want to spend any more money on a house that has already been draining them. However, in many cases it will be necessary to dip into savings to get a house sold.

If you're short on cash and need to get the house sold to cash out your equity, you may need to look at other sources.

Money in Retirement Account

If you have money in a 401k, Individual Retirement Account (IRA) or other retirement account, you can take some of this out if it will get you a sufficient return on your investment. If you take money out of your retirement account prematurely, you'll pay a 10 percent penalty, plus income tax on the distribution. Even so, if you can get a 100 percent return on your money invested, it may be worth the penalty and taxes. If it's costing you thousands of dollars each month in mortgage payments, insurance, and utilities, the bite may be worth it to take out the money and get your house sold faster. Review the options with your tax professional before proceeding.

Credit Cards and Credit Lines

You may already have more available credit than you realize. Credit cards and other existing revolving debt accounts can be quite useful in real estate investing. Most major credit cards allow you to take cash advances or write checks to borrow on the account. The transaction fees and interest rates are fairly high, but you can access this money on 24-hour notice. Also, you won't have to pay loan costs normally associated with a real estate transaction, such as title insurance, appraisals, pest inspections, surveys, and so forth. Often, you will be better off paying 18 percent interest or more on a credit line for three months than paying 7 percent interest on an institutional loan, which has thousands of dollars in upfront costs that would take you years to recoup.

Promotional interest rates are often available on your credit cards, but again, beware. These rates often skyrocket after several months. The chances are that if you have a favorable credit history, you will be able to raise your credit limits on your existing cards. High-interest debt must be approached cautiously, and your personality type may not embrace the idea of tens of thousands of dollars in revolving debt. However, avoiding mortgages can be helpful in saving time and often money for short-term borrowing, so keep credit cards in mind. You can also benefit by using store cards with no cash advance features. These cards are available through all the major lumberyards, hardware-store chains, and home-improvement stores. They'll allow you to finance your materials costs that can involve many thousands of dollars.

Using a Home Equity Line of Credit

A home equity line of credit (HELOC) can be an excellent financing tool, if it's used properly. A HELOC is basically a credit card secured by a mortgage or deed of trust on your property. You only pay interest on the amount you borrow on the HELOC. If you don't use the line of credit, you don't have any monthly payments to make. You can access the HELOC by writing checks provided by the lender. In most cases, it will be a second lien on your property.

Bring in a Partner

Bringing in a partner is a good way to start if you're flat broke and lack experience in renovating houses. But choose your partners carefully. Don't pick a partner because he's your friend or you think it would be fun to complete a business deal together. Choose a partner with money and rehab experience in real estate that can fix up the property and get it sold. You can split the profits, that is, the difference between what you owe and what the property eventually sells for—less commission, closing costs, and the cost of materials. Do the math carefully, and consider what it might cost to hire a contractor versus partnering.

Painting Party

If you're really strapped for cash and have a few loyal friends, throw a painting party. Invite over some friends for some pizza and a beer or soda to help you paint the house. Words of advice—most people are pretty sloppy painters, so do the prep work in advance. Cover the furniture, tape the corners, and place the drop clothes on the carpets before you start.

Chapter Summary

- You need to get your house looking its best before you offer it to market.

- If your house has already been on the market, take it off, clean it up a little, try a fresh coat of paint, and stage it so that it looks unforgettable.

- Refer to the checklist of rehabbing and staging tips in the resource directory of this program.

CHAPTER 5

The Best Offense
Is a Good Defense—
Getting Your
Information Organized

A first-rate organizer is never in a hurry. He is never late. He always keeps up his sleeve a margin for the unexpected.

—Enoch Arnold Bennett

Before you bring your house to market, you'll have to get your information organized and your ducks in a row. There are two parts to organization that we discuss in this chapter. The first is specifically relevant to your property and the documents relevant to the sale. Delay on the seller's part is the number one reason that deals often fall apart. This chapter will also discuss how to organize the information you have researched and convey it to the people who are likely to be interested in buying your house. If your supply quotient (see Chapter 2) is greater than six, the sooner you can get your buyer to sign on the line that is dotted, the more likely it is you will achieve the highest possible price.

What's Up Doc?

The following is a list of 10 important documents that will help you close your transaction smoothly:

1. **Deed.** You will need a copy of your deed for a variety of reasons, not the least of which is to know the exact legal description of your property. The legal description is generally inserted into the contract of sale. In addition, you may need to refer to your deed for easements, restrictions and other criteria.

2. **Survey.** A survey shows the boundaries of your property and how they relate to the improvements upon them. If any issue arises regarding the fence line or any encroachments, the survey will be useful to straighten out these issues.

3. **Title policy.** Your title insurance policy you purchased when you bought the property may come in handy if there are any issues involving title to the property that need to be resolved before the closing. If so, you can contact the title insurer who issued to policy and look for indemnity for these issues.

4. **Certificate of completion.** If you had any work done on the property that required permits, a certificate of completion for each item will be necessary to show your buyer and the appraiser.

5. **HOA and CCRs.** Copies of any homeowners' association declarations and any conditions, covenants, or restrictions on the use of the property will need to be provided to your buyer.

6. **List of schools.** Your deal could live or die by the school systems, so make sure you have all of the information about public schools ready for your prospective buyer.

7. **Warranties and owner's manuals.** Gather all of the warranties and owner's manuals for appliances, roof, electrical, sprinkler systems, and so forth.

8. **Service contracts.** If you have any service contracts for your heating and ventilation systems, security systems, or other items, keep these handy, especially if they are transferrable.

9. **Tax and utility bills.** Copies of your most recent property tax and utility bills would be extremely relevant to the sale of your property, so make sure you have this information handy for your buyers.

10. **Insurance policies.** Copies of any insurance policies and bills to be able to quote rates to your buyer will be helpful.

Creating a Killer Flyer

Most real estate agents use a printout from the MLS which is infor-mation-based, not a sales piece. The flier should not be simply fea-tures and benefits, but a true sales piece that appeals to people's emotions. Boring headlines like "Just Listed" or "Large 4BR/2BA" only appeal to people's intellect. People buy with emotion, so use headlines like, "Imagine Your Family Living Here for Christmas" or "What a Valentine's Gift This Will Be." Have a peek at your competition's fliers for ideas.

Unpack Your Adjectives

Try to make your descriptions just a little rosier than your competi-tion. For example, if they say, "master bedroom," you say, "master bedroom suite." If they say, "Master Bedroom Suite," you say, "Honeymoon Master Bedroom Suite." If they say, "Honeymoon Master Bedroom Suite," you say "Honeymoon Master Bedroom Suite with Imported Tile." You get the idea!

Flattering Photos Are the Key

Since the photo on your listing is your first impression, make sure it's a good one. If you don't have a good digital camera, then borrow one from a friend. A digital single-lens reflex (SLR) camera with an interchangeable lens is your best bet. If you only have one house to sell, the recommended camera is the Kodak V705, which has both a regular and wide angle lens and retails for under $200 on eBay.

Lighting is the key to a good photograph. A good flash with a wide-angle lens works better than natural light for indoor shots. If you're unsure of the best angle to use when you photograph a room, start with the entryway. Most of us decorate from the entryway, whether we realize it or not. Stand in the doorway of each room and snap a couple of angles facing in. If you have a special focal point in the room, like a fireplace or nice view, take a picture facing that object. Show the buyers what their view would be if they sat at the breakfast table and looked out over the yard. Show them what they'd see if they sat facing the fireplace. If there's no furniture in the room, borrow some attractive pieces to make the picture look good. If the pictures look good, the buyer will get hooked, even if he knows deep down the furniture isn't included.

Make sure you have exterior pictures that reflect the current season. If it begins snowing while you're selling, retake your exterior pictures and swap them out. Having pictures that don't reflect the seasons gives the impression of a house that's been lingering on the market. And you should always show your house at its best. If your flower beds begin to bloom, take new pictures that reflect the garden's glory. It could be a selling point to the right buyer.

Believe it or not, a sunny day makes it more difficult to take pictures outside because it casts shadows on the house. You are better off taking pictures on an overcast day or early in the morning. If the sky looks dull in the picture, use a software program like Adobe Photoshop to make the sky look blue. If your grass is dull or has brown spots in the photo, crop them out so the lawn looks beautiful.

The Power of Virtual Curb Appeal. The latest trend of buyers is to initially eliminate the homes they don't like simply based on the way it looks on the Internet. It's uncanny how often the virtual curb appeal of the home affects the decision-making process of the buyer. You, as the seller, can capitalize tremendously on this phenomenon by improving the curb appeal of the home with a landscaper from the vantage point of the street. For example, if there are trees blocking the view of the home, try to trim them back from the bottom up until the majority of the home can be viewed from the street. Obviously, a well-proportioned amount of seasonal shrubbery and foliage is appropriate.

To show the physical appearance of the home, a good photograph that is touched up a little can dramatically improve the virtual appeal of the home. For example, a blue sky with white, fluffy clouds can be added to the photo. Slightly enhance the coloring and contrast of the lawn, roof, and siding, and make the photo more brilliantly appealing. Make sure your curb-appeal photo and web site are better, prettier, and more striking than the dozen nearest competitors to your house.

Crop the photo of your home proportionally so the house is 75 to 85 percent of the photo; otherwise it will appear small. Many times, the perception of the buyer is misled by a large house that appears in a photo taken from far away.

The 80-20 Angle

The ideal angle of the photo is not dead on, but rather taken at an angle at which you can see 20 percent of the side of the house. This will give the photo a three-dimensional look and more depth. Naturally, the better side of the home should be taken with emphasis to capturing amenities in the rear of the home, such as garages, pools, and swing sets.

The best side of the home should come first. Occasionally, the rear view of the home showing off the yard and decking would be the better choice, particularly in the case of a walkout basement.

First Things First—Prioritizing Photos and Features

Once you've taken a wide variety of pictures, sort them by importance. You should have one main picture, usually the best picture of the front of your house. Your second photo should be of the kitchen, which is the most important room in the house (assuming, of course, that your kitchen looks good!). The third most important room is the master bathroom. Then pick other favorites that you can use on your flyers or Internet sites. Pick pictures that show off the most important architectural features or things that make your house special. Don't be afraid to choose a picture of your tray ceiling over one of your living rooms. Those special details are what get buyers interested. Once they're hooked, they can see the rest of the house in person.

If you don't have good photos or enough fliers to show off your home, get some pictures of the neighborhood. Local attractions, parks, beaches, golf courses, shopping centers, or schools are good choices. If there's nothing much to show, use some stock images you can download for a few bucks on the Internet (at www.istock photo.com or www.bigstockphoto.com).

The clearest and most concise bullet points, arranged in order of value, tend to be the most comprehensive format for buyers to remember. The whole point of this marketing is to motivate and stand out from the competition. The overwhelming amount of information that buyers receive dilutes their focus and often makes the home-buying process painful and tedious. Our objective is to convey the greatest features first, followed by motivation for buyers to take action to attend a viewing of the property as soon as possible.

A Drop of Blood Brings Attention from All the Fish . . .

Buyers want to get a deal, so convince them you're motivated to give a deal. Specifically, use words like, MUST SELL, FORECLOSURE (if you are in foreclosure), STEAL MY HOUSE, FIRST REASONABLE OFFER, LISTED UNDER MARKET, or SAY HELLO TO A GOOD BUY. You don't necessarily have to give your house away, but the point is to get the attention of as many buyers are possible. Remember, it's a numbers game. You have the true knowledge of what your property is worth because you have done your due diligence; it's right there in black and white in your comp book, supported by your personal inspection of the competition. Furthermore, this can all be documented and proven to your potential buyer when the time is right, typically at the end of the negotiation process. Please note, the price you are willing to accept for this home should be the *last* thing you talk about with the buyers after you have reviewed with them all of the features of your property and how they compare to the comps you will hand pick and show to the buyer to make your point.

Highest and Best Use Theory

Develop your flier with the most likely buyer in mind. If your likely buyer is a family, focus on the schools, the finished basement, and the local parks. If your likely buyer is a retired couple, focus on the local hospitals, the quiet neighborhood, and the fact that it's a ranch with no stairs. The comp book will leave many clues as to the most likely buyer for your property. If you're not sure, drive by the most recently sold properties and get an idea of the people who are living there.

Map

People pass out your flyers to their friends, so make sure there's a map on the flier with a route leading to your house. Web sites such as Google, Mapquest, and Yahoo have printable maps you can copy and paste onto your flier.

Create a Web Site

Setting up a web site is easier, cheaper and faster than ever! A dedicated web site with your home address ("234MainStreet.com") is a great way to give a detailed look at your houses to your buyers. A web site is a great way to give potential buyers a view of your house without getting into their car or being intimidated by an agent or a high-pressure salesperson. You can mention the web site in your MLS listing, your fliers, your sign, and any other advertising.

If you have a high-priced house, it might be worth it to invest in a virtual tour. There are services such as www.360house.com that use special camera techniques to take 360-degree images of your rooms. You can imbed the multimedia into your dedicated web site. Potential buyers can watch these mini-videos and imagine that they're standing in the center of each room and looking all around. It can be a powerful sales tool! If you have a good video camera and good lighting, a short, professionally narrated Internet clip on YouTube can really make things come alive!

A list of affordable web-site options can be found in the resource directory of this book. If you're a complete neophyte when it comes to web sites and technology, consider placing an ad or looking in the services section of the Internet classified provider craigslist.org for a local high school or college kid who can help you out for a reasonable fee.

Tools of the Trade

There are certain tools of the trade to help you sell the property faster and should be seen as essential, especially if you have several properties or are an agent regularly selling properties.

The 7-Eleven stores don't lock their doors because they're always open for business. We can't emphasize enough how important it is to make sure there is constant access to your property for buyers. Some homeowners put limitations on when the property can be shown such as "By appointment only." This is the greatest hindrance that sellers can inflict on themselves that is within their control. If someone knocks on the door on Sunday at 7 P.M., you show the property! You should be ready to show the property whether or not the beds are made.

A buyer's motivation to knock on your door when you least expect it will far outweigh any negative implications of your house being less than perfectly in order. Buyers want to find the best possible home and often won't come back for a second look once they are at the house. Remember, they're in a process-of-elimination mode and just want to get through their whole list of available options. It's more often the case that buyers will move on to viewing more houses than to come back to yours. So, it would be wiser to be prepared at almost any time, since you will never really know when the best possible buyer for your house will show up. Like fishing, it's the element of the unknown. Being prepared for the unknown will highly increase your odds, especially since a buyer who shows up at your house at 7 P.M. on a Sunday with his wife and children is probably very motivated to buy! Why lose that opportunity?

Some of our best buying candidates come around at the end of the weekend—when they're tired, confused, and simply want to get done with finding a home for their family. Interestingly enough, the same home shown first versus last has less of a chance since buyers today are compelled to turn up every stone and look at every house on the market. If we have a choice of when to show our homes, we would certainly want to be the *last* home on the list. Many professional agents know this fact and use it to their advantage in trying to direct a buyer to a particular property that they feel is the best value for this buyer. It's not uncommon for agents to intentionally show homes they know are not suitable or a value for the buyer, then show the best value for the buyer last, so that they can then logically proceed and move the buyer onto the negotiation process.

The Lockbox

A lockbox is an important tool for your success, because it gives you availability to your property 24/7 for showings. In fact, three sets of keys aside from the lockbox should be on hand for showing the property. Since access to the property is one of the easiest things for the seller to control and can have the greatest effect on the ultimate selling price on the home, more is better. It's not uncommon for an agent to pick up a set of keys in advance of showing the property while another buyer wants to see the property at the same time. Again, buyers often don't come back for a second try when there are so many choices for them to choose from where they don't have to wait or be inconvenienced.

The keys should be for the front door or entryway of the property, not the back door or garage, which is not where you generally want your buyer to come into the house first.

iPhone, Your Phone, Any Phone Will Do

If you have a phone number on your fliers, make sure it's a cellular number where you or some other live person can respond immediately. The timeliness of callbacks is critical to your success. Buyers will typically make their schedule for appointments for the weekend on a Thursday or Friday. Once their schedule is filled, they'll put you off until the following weekend, and so you risk losing the buyer to another house they saw. If you can't answer the phone live, forward it to a 24/7 live answering service, such as PAT Live (www.patlive.com).

Bigger Is Better

Keep a large measuring tape in the home (cloth type, so you don't scratch furniture). This will allow your potential buyers to physically measure the rooms. The subtle benefit of this device is to help slow down the showing process and to keep the buyer in the home longer, allowing you to interact more on a personal level. Remember, it's all about the buyers—this would be a good opportunity to ask them about their wants, needs, and desires. The second great benefit is you can often tell who (husband or wife) is more in charge, based on your observations of watching them interact with each other. For example, it may be that the leader of the two will take charge with the tape measure. Or the detail-oriented of the two will grab the tape. Either way, you'll observe how they work together and think. Lastly, if they measure every room in the house, you know you've got a live one!

Planning for Success

Have your pocket planner in hand as you ask for another appointment. If buyers are not inclined to come back again, this may be a sign that they aren't interested. However, if they quickly agree to another showing, this is without a doubt an interested buyer. At this point, great care should be taken not to do something to turn the buyer off. We highly recommend you accommodate any timeframe that works for them. Allow them to come back again with any relatives or friends. Rarely do buyers buy without bringing the real estate maven. The ultimate negotiations in price usually turn on the maven's opinion of the property. Block out a minimum of two hours for the maven. The time you choose to show the property is crucial, too. For example, if a local business or church causes traffic or parking problems during a certain time period, make sure you don't show the property at that time. We'll discuss the maven in more detail in the chapter on negotiations.

Post-Its to Post It

Carry brightly colored post-it notes to mark a spot of the house that may need attention (such as touch up paint) such as a staging touch, a repair of sorts, or as a reminder to whomever to lock up doors behind them and turn off lights. Occasionally post-its can be used to point out features, such as specific upgrades that aren't obvious, such as an electric box upgrades, new appliances, or sprinkler systems. Think of the car dealer who headlines the features of the car in the window with a sticker. It should be simple and clear.

Streetwise Navigation Systems

As you're doing your due diligence and driving around looking at houses, a relatively inexpensive navigation system will be your best friend and save you hours of time. Some systems have the ability to route your address entries in an efficient and fuel-saving manner. Driving around with a virtual assistant guiding your way will allow you to focus on the comps rather than the direction, allowing you to get the best value calculations. If you are really tight for cash, a laminated *Hagstrom* map and a washable marker are a good second choice.

Signs of the Times

A yard sign is one of the most common ways a buyer will find your house. Make sure your sign is large and legible from the street. Avoid cheap, generic signs and go with a metal-framed sign, which you'll find at a real estate supply store or web site. Make sure your sign has both a phone number and web site address listed for more information. You can even print a custom sign in full color with photos of the inside of the house. Use solar lighting near the sign so that it glows at night, making it a 24/7 billboard for your property!

Make sure you have a place where people can grab an information flier, usually attached to the sign itself. Avoid the cheap info-tubes that will mangle your flier; instead use the larger boxes that can hold a good number of fliers. A complete list of realtor-supply web sites can be found in the web site resource directory in Appendix J of this book. Make sure you tape one flier to the inside of the flyer box in case it runs out. Make friends with neighbors that have children and offer them a $20 incentive to have their children keep a watch to make sure the flier box is always full. Nothing is more tragic than an empty flyer box, when a potential buyer stops at your house!

If the house is vacant and the front lawn is not large, put the flier box on the stoop of the house by the front door. Have a big, obvious arrow pointing from the sign to the front door with the words MORE INFO. Tape a flier to the inside of the screen door window. If there is no screen door, tape it inside the front windows.

Directional signs in your neighborhood are extremely effective for getting traffic to your house, particularly if it's not on a main street. Check and replace these signs often, because the wind or a competitor may remove them. If local zoning prohibits using signs, here's a tip. Place them on Friday afternoon and remove them by Sunday evening, because code-enforcement officers usually don't work on weekends! Be aware that some localities may give a fine for using these signs so check with your local municipalities. Generally observe what others are doing—if builders are placing signs out on the weekends in your neighborhood and are getting away with it, so will you. In short, use your signs judiciously—don't overdo it.

Place signs at the main entrances to the neighborhood and at as many heavy traffic intersections as possible within a certain radius of the property. For example, all major intersections north, south, east, and west should direct traffic to your house. Make sure not to block sidewalks or place signs on medians, blocking traffic signs. Red-and-white lettering stands out the most, and make sure your phone number is large enough to read on the sign. Carry a variety of styles of signs, so that you can adapt your strategy to the type of location in which the sign will be placed. For example, some signs have metal stakes that go into the dirt and are easy to install. Heavy duty, wind-resistant metal-framed signs are more appropriate for a place with concrete. A telephone pole or large tree is excellent for smaller signs that can be placed up high using a sign stapler (www.signstapler.com).

Keeping in Orbit. "Orbit" was the nickname we gave to the person responsible for making sure our directional signs didn't get knocked down by wind, accident, or another competitor. Most weekend traffic comes from strategically placed directional signs that have a habit of blowing over if placed near another directional sign. Have a person who can drive around on a regular basis to make sure the signs you place are still there and are replaced on a regular basis.

Contract

If you live in an area where real estate contracts are not generally prepared by attorneys, make sure you have a copy of the customary contracts that real estate agents use. You don't have to be a legal expert, but make sure you understand the basics of the contract, and learn how to fill one out. If you have a buyer that is ready to go, the worst thing you can do is put him off because you don't know how to take a deposit and fill out a contract.

In areas where attorneys commonly prepare contracts, a binder agreement is sometimes used. A binder is like a deposit that reserves the property for a few days while you take it off the market for the buyer. It's not the same as a formal contract, but operates like a short-term option. The bottom line is not really the contract or binder itself but rather the commitment of the buyer, both financially and emotionally. Once buyers express interest in your property, you must do whatever it takes to get that commitment in writing. If binders are not commonly used in your area, then make sure your attorney is available immediately following the meeting of the minds.

Calculator

A rent-versus-own calculator is a good tool to show your potential buyers the true net cost to their investment, since it takes into account the huge tax benefits that most buyers fail to recognize. The compounded effect of these benefits, plus the savings of rent and reduction of principal on their mortgage cannot be overstated. However, these benefits are the most underappreciated part of the negotiation process in the buyer's mind. At the proper time, this tool is best to use to close the sale and then agree to a price both parties can accept. Using the computations of several price points in the calculator will be a great visual aid to the buyer to prove that the investment makes relative sense, since the additional monies that we typically need from the buyer to make the deal are normally insignificant when compared to the overall investment as an aggregate.

This tool can be obtained online here:

http://realestate.yahoo.com/calculators/rent_vs_own.html

Print out various scenarios based on price assumptions that you can give your prospective buyers, so that they can use this as justification for meeting your price. The psychologist effect in the buyer's mind is to place him in the position of actual home ownership vicariously through the responsibility of making a proposed mortgage payment. In a way, it's like getting a consumer into a car for a test drive. The whole idea is to get the buyer to appreciate that the monthly investment is less than what it appears to be because of the added tax benefits, principal reduction, and inevitable market appreciation that real estate enjoys over the long term. Furthermore, pride of home ownership is something we all seek; it is only the numbers that hold us back. This tool can make or break the marginal transaction in which a buyer needs that extra push to get over the fence. Since we all need a push once in a while, factual data in writing can help overcome the number one objection, which is the price.

The I's Have It! Imagination and Initiative

The best tools of the trade are free—use your imagination and initiative. While doing your due diligence, you will come across ideas that may seem strange. Some ideas may seem brilliant, some may seem downright stupid. All of these should be jotted down in a 3-by-5-inch notebook that you should carry with you at all times, since the integration of a successful transaction and your lifestyle will need to become one. Since this business is a 24/7 operation, the best ideas come when you're least expecting them.

Chapter Summary

- Get your information organized and ready for your potential buyers.
- Know your tools of the trade.

CHAPTER 6

Choose the Right Agent or Sell It Yourself— Which Is Right for You?

The broker sold me a two-story house. I got the first story before I bought it and the second story after I moved in.

—Anonymous

Before you put your house on the market you need to decide whether to use a real estate agent or sell it on your own. The answer to this question will depend on a lot of factors, as we will discuss. Although this chapter is about choosing whether to sell with an agent or on your own, the bottom line is how you are going to get the best customer through your door to buy your house. This is a function of how much exposure and how effective the exposure on your house is. It takes time and expertise to maximize the exposure of the property to the largest and most qualified audience. A good real estate broker does have some advantages over a for sale by owner. However, with the right strategies and guidance, giving it a try on your own is worth it, assuming you have the time, money, and few key support people to help you through the process.

Before we start this chapter, let's get our mindset adjusted correctly. The goal here is very simple: it's a matter of finding one single buying unit—single, couple, or family. We need just one, but the aim is to the get the one that is the *best*, that is, the one who can give you the highest price and the best terms, to close within your time frame.

So before we discuss whether to use an agent or to go it on your own, we will first discuss what kind of customer we are looking for and the different ways we will find these customers.

It's All About the Customer (RAW)

Going back to the discussion in Chapter 1, finding a buyer is all a numbers game. We're going to go through a lot of potential lookers to find a buyer who is "ready, able, and willing" (or RAW). The rule of thumb is that 100 buyers will need to look at your home (either drive by or view on the Internet) before you get 10 interested buyers. These 10 interested buyers should be defined as either very serious lookers or people who have made offers. Very serious lookers are people who spend a significant chunk of time viewing the property or, preferably, have come back to look for a second time, either by themselves or with their real estate maven. Anyone who made an offer, even a low-ball, is better than a window shopper and falls into our magical category of 10. From this pool of 10, there should be the one, highest, and best user of the property who is ready, able, and willing to pay you the highest possible price for that property and to close the deal.

"Got To" Versus "Want To"

While screening your buyers, keep an eye out for the highest and best one. There's a distinction amongst buyers that a seller should keep in mind. Some buyers want to buy and some *have* to buy. It's the filtering of these buyers that will determine the effort and focus that a seller should place on the prospect. For example, buyers who have sold their home and must buy within their contractual obligation, which they have committed to when they sold their property, would be considered golden buyers. Assuming their qualifications and needs fall within the range of value that your property offers, then these buyers should receive the greatest amount of effort and focus.

Not all buyers are created equal—it is the motivation of the buyer that is the paramount distinction between buyers. A buyer who simply wants to buy but doesn't really have to buy has proven to be one of the greatest time wasters and disappointments for sellers. So, understanding these criteria will make the rest of the screening process easy. Where there is little desire, a low offer usually follows.

Where Do They Come From?

Where do the best buyers come from? It depends on your marketplace. Usually this can be determined in large part from looking at your comps book. Right in the book itself you will learn not only what people paid for houses like yours, but the terms they paid and their names and where they moved from. If you are using a good real estate broker (who has read this book), she should contact the selling and listing agents of properties like yours that have recently sold or opened escrow.

The seven main sources from which the best buyers typically come are discussed in the pages that follow:

The Person Who Sold a Home, Who Needs to Buy a Home.

These buyers are the *best* buyers, since they have the highest level of motivation. They're moving out of a house shortly, because they're required by contract to do so. Keeping this in mind, it is also good to keep in mind how you can accommodate their time frame. So the logical question to ask such a buyer is, "When do you have to move out of your current house?" The buyer may not want to give you this information, but very often we have found that when asked this question at the right time and in the right way (when rapport has been established), buyers will spill the beans and tell you the time frame they are working within. These particular buyers are owed as many follow up calls as possible since they may be looking at your property in the earliest part of their shopping process.

Until buyers have truly shopped and compared available homes in the marketplace, it's hard for them to make a decision about which home suits them best. So asking *any* buyers how many homes they have looked at and over what period of time is the quickest and most efficient way to determine how ready they are to buy. For example, studies have shown that the average buyer takes about 10 full shopping days within the time frame of 1 to 6 months. Depending on the available inventory in the marketplace, they would normally physically inspect between one and three dozen homes. This does not include the screening process that is done online prior to the actual visit. Once they have completed their list of possibilities, buyers often need to be reminded of the properties they saw early in the process. Offering a second showing as a refresher to the buyer has resulted in many successful sales. Studies have shown that buyers will typically prefer to purchase homes at the end of a week-end of shopping, normally followed up by a one more time look at the home that we've been referring to as the "re-show."

The last thoughts we have on this topic are that you can really never judge a book by its cover, but if you know what the odds are, you'll know when to press your luck and persist and when to back off and leave a buyer alone. Sometimes, the hardest part of a trans-action is selling an appointment for a re-show and coordinating the key decision makers, which at this point you have hopefully learned are the wife and her mother. Husbands, of course, will have the power of the veto, but if these are families you're working with, Momma has a whole lot to say about the final decision. Studies have shown that among the overwhelming majority of families who buy homes, the wife tends to do most of the shopping and tends to find the house first.

From Real Estate Brokers Who Had Customers Who Lost Out on a Home to Another Bidder.   One of our favorite sce-narios is the Runaway Bride syndrome. This is the case where the buyer has, for whatever reason, just lost out on purchasing a home similar to yours because of a better offer from another buyer. Typi-cally, it was a higher offer, but it could have been someone more qualified to buy. Regardless of the circumstances, this buyer is now ripe to purchase a home. We cherish these scenarios, because such people are ready, able, and willing (and a little brokenhearted). They know what they want, and they've learned that they're not the only buyers in the market. This is why the comp book has so much weight and effect because it's a show-and-tell aide to relieve the buyers from the fear that they're paying too much for your home, when in fact other homes like yours have just sold for the same amount or more. It's always a good idea to show them the *best* comps first, especially if their curb appeal photo is inferior to yours.

One last thought—it would be interesting to find out why they were not the successful bidders on the last transaction. Asking the buyer why will give you their version of the story. That would give you clues as to how to frame your negotiation around these particular buyers. The one thing we have learned is that no two real estate transactions are ever the same. However, the underlying common denominators of both parties tend to vary only slightly. The buyer just wants to find a nice home for his family that he feels is a fair value in today's market. Naturally, the buyer would like to get the best possible price, but when it comes to single-family homes, the emotional factors normally outweigh the logic. So sell with the sizzle and close with the facts that you will now have on hand from your comp book, your best tool for closing the deal.

Mortgage Brokers Who Have Prequalified a Buyer. Mortgage brokers often have a list of clients they have prequalified for a loan either because they called from an ad in the paper or radio, or were qualified for another house that fell through for whatever reason. Or it could be that the buyers could not qualify for a $300,000 home they put an offer on, but they are qualified for your $250,000 home. Either way, mortgage brokers only get paid when the loan is closed, and so they're happy to share with you a list of qualified buyers before another mortgage broker and real estate agent team take them away.

Friends and Relatives of People Who Bought Homes in Your Area. In your comps book, you should have a list of the most recent sales of homes most like yours and closest to yours in location and price. At the very least, these new homeowners should be invited to your open house, since they are obviously satisfied consumers of a similar product. People who have just bought a large-ticket item love to brag to all their friends and relatives about how wonderful a decision they've made. Naturally, we'd love to capitalize on their new-found enthusiasm, while they are still on the ether! Leaving them about a dozen color fliers clearly indentifying the date and time of your Grand Opening Open House should be delivered at least one weekend in advance. This gives your top prospective salespeople a chance to distribute your information over the week to their closest friends and relatives who are considering a similar move.

Families Expanding Who Need a Larger Home. Occasionally, local contractors can be a great source of leads, since they often deal with families who are considering making the colossal mistake of over-improving their home for the neighborhood. Eventually, when reality sets in, they realize that moving into a larger home makes more sense. Local landscapers and the mail carriers should be given a handful of fliers with perhaps a small incentive to distribute them amongst their immediate network of local contacts.

Tenants Whose Leases Are Up and Want to Stop Paying Rent.

Dense and sparsely populated apartment buildings and condominiums can be a great source of prospective buyers with growing families. Simply leave a stack of fliers in an apartment lobby or condo building. If there is a community bulletin board or newsletter in the complex, try and get your flier into these avenues.

Empty-Nesters with Bigger Homes Who Want to Trade Down.

Owners of homes that are obviously much larger than yours and are close in proximity may be potential buyers for your home. You can purchase a list of people in the proximity of your home that are in a neighborhood of larger homes who have owned them for 10 years or more. Try an Internet data provider (www.infousa.com). Odds are they're empty-nesters, or are shortly becoming so, and want to move down in size.

Home Inspectors Who Inspected a Home That the Prospective Buyer Didn't Buy.

Real estate transactions often fail because of an inspection item. Inspectors might be able to share information about these potential buyers. A list of local home inspectors is relatively easy to obtain via the Internet (www.ashi.org or www.nashi.org). Stop by their office and offer some fliers of your property with the idea that they may have contact with very active buyers who are still in the market for a home.

1031 Exchange Buyers.

Under section 1031 of the Internal Revenue Code, an investor can sell a property and buy a replacement property without paying capital gains tax. While the rules are rather technical and beyond the scope of this book, suffice it to say that such a buyer is under duress to buy a replacement property or risk adverse tax consequences. Contact local 1031 exchange facilitators and let them know you have a property for sale and you will be flexible to work within their parameters and timeframes. Ask them for a list of potential buyers, or, at the very least, give them a set of your property flyers. You can find a list of local exchange facilitators by searching Yahoo Local or Google GOOG-411.

Thinking Outside the Box. We once had a house in a suburban area that was on such a busy street that nobody would even consider looking at the inside. In fact, the owner had had several pets killed in front of the house over the years due to the high volume and speed of traffic. The owner tried selling his home for years with no success.

We took an unconventional approach and decided to market the home to potential buyers who lived on busy streets who might not mind the high-traffic area. We compiled a list of homes under contract for sale on busy streets in a nearby urban area. One particular prospect, Rocco, showed interest and viewed our home for sale. After touring the inside of the home, Rocco held his wife's hand, took a deep breath, and said to his wife as trucks barreled down the street, "Honey, I just love the country!" It's all a matter of perspective—Rocco happened to live on the service road of a six-lane major highway and had become oblivious to the traffic.

What Can They Afford?

It's a good idea to establish a relationship with a mortgage broker before you begin the sales process. The subjects that most buyers are leery about are their credit and their ability to get a loan. However, you can't sell your house unless they face these fears. Call a few mortgage brokers, and find one that you're comfortable with. Tell them you're selling a home and you want to be able to refer potential buyers to them. This way, you can tell your potential buyers that you know a person who would be glad to talk with them about their credit and their ability to pay—and she's a nice person!

Mortgage brokers provide two important services—prequalification and preapproval. When a buyer comes to one of your showings and says he's prequalified, that's a good start. However, what you really want is preapproval. To get prequalified, the buyer has to sit down with a lender and give his side of the story: How much he makes in a week, how much debt he has, what monthly payments he already has to make, other expenses, and so forth. Then the mortgage broker nails down a sum of money for which the buyer should be able to get approved.

This is only half the story—what about a credit check? What about verification of employment, and so forth? In a prequalification, the lender simply takes the buyer's word for it. Prequalifications are nonbinding and are offered free of charge by most mortgage lenders. They can't go to the expense of pulling a buyer's credit report or calling his employer to make sure he's legit—that's what preapproval is for.

Preapproval typically entails a full analysis on the buyers' financial situation. Mortgage brokers will run a credit check on the applicants, ask for pay stubs and tax returns, look at copies of their bills, and assess their overall credit-worthiness. After this process, the lender will issue a preapproval letter. This will show a dollar amount that the buyer is guaranteed to be able to borrow—so long as the underlying property is worth the asking price.

Since the subprime meltdown, the preapproval letter must be as current as possible because changes in the credit markets will affect ability to pay. It also might indicate how long ago the buyers started shopping for a home and how qualified they are. For example, if the letter is six months old, you'd want to know why—is there some other issue holding them back? So, before you lose your highest and best buyer to what we call the wannabe buyer, make sure you've done your due diligence concerning this buyer's ability to close. It does take some experience to tell the real from the fake buyer, since many times buyers may stay tight-lipped about how badly they truly want your property. We will discuss how to test the buyer's level of sincerity and motivation in the chapter on negotiations.

Trying It on Your Own

Although most properties are eventually sold through real estate agents, statistics show that the majority of buyers initially find their desired property through the Internet, a yard sign, a newspaper ad, a drive-by, or a referral. Thus, the ultimate goal would be to zero in on finding the best buyer on your own, provided that you have the time and resources to market and manage the transaction properly. While this may be the ideal scenario, it may not always be the practical result, so using a real estate agent, or broker, may be a necessary part of the transaction, as we will discuss later in this chapter. Assuming you're willing to do 90 percent of what we have discussed, then you might attempt to sell your home on your own for one to three weekends, not counting holidays. Your chance of con-necting with the best possible buyer on your own will diminish ex-ponentially past the third weekend. In fact, studies have shown that after the third weekend, you are now wasting time and money, and would be far better off by stepping up your marketing efforts to the next level and hiring a professional.

If you have the time and effort to run your own open houses and meet with buyers and agents on relatively short notice every day of the week, then you may consider using a broker who will give you the expertise to help you at a discounted commission, provided that you do all the leg work. This arrangement can usually be upgraded later to a full service agency if you can't sell it on your own. The idea here is to save money by using the broker's expertise yet get a big discount on the fee since you are doing the leg work. We will dis-cuss later in this chapter.

The Basics of Brokers

A person must be licensed as a real estate broker or agent to list property. A listing is an agreement between the seller and the broker that permits the broker or agent to sell the property for a fee. In most cases, this fee is about 6 percent of the sales price, paid at closing when the sale is complete. The broker or agent who signs this agree-ment with the seller is called the "listing broker" or "listing agent."

The difference between an agent and a broker is a licensing distinc-tion. The state licensing authority requires that at least one person in the real estate office have a broker's license. In most states, in order to achieve the status of broker, one must have achieved a higher level of educational and transactional experience and pass a broker's exam.

An agent (also known as a "salesperson") is licensed to sell real es-tate, but is required to work under a licensed broker. The licensed broker (also known as "broker of record," "broker in charge," or "principal broker") of the office is responsible for the actions of other agents in her office. Sometimes those agents may also be licensed brokers as well, hence the expression "broker associate." These broker associates have also achieved a higher level of educational experience than just real estate agents, but are not responsible for the actions of other brokers and agents in the office. While a broker and an agent are different, we often refer to them synonymously throughout this book as "agent," as in someone who is licensed to sell real estate.

Seller's Broker versus Buyer's Broker

Brokers can represent buyers or sellers in different capacities. Traditionally, there was one type of broker, a seller's (aka "listing") broker, whose allegiance and fiduciary were to the seller. The broker who took the listing on the property would find a buyer and get paid his commission from the proceeds of the sale of the property from the seller. The listing broker will typically employ the agents of his office, other offices, and their agents to all act on behalf of the seller. Even agents that work intimately with a buyer under this traditional arrangement still owe their loyalty and fiduciary to the seller. An agent or broker who sells a property on behalf of the listing broker and/or seller is called a "subagent."

In more recent years, brokers have taken another role, that of representing the buyer's interest ("buyer's broker" or "buyer's agency"). A buyer's broker owes a fiduciary responsibility to the buyer. If the seller's broker offers a co-operation fee to a buyer's broker's agency, the commission is split between the seller's broker and the buyer's broker. For example, if a property is sold for $100,000 and the sellers' broker's commission is 6 percent, the buyer's broker would get $3,000, and the seller's broker would get $3,000. The seller would net $94,000, less any other closing costs in the transaction. Although the commission split in the preceding example was fifty-fifty, the seller's broker can negotiate for more or less with the buyer's broker. If there is no cooperative agreement, the buyer is responsible for paying his own broker.

Agency Disclosure

Make sure you get a written explanation of the broker or agent's relationship with you. Who do they represent, who is going to pay them, and what are your obligations if you buy a property without them? Each state has different ways of handling the agency relationship. The laws of agency are constantly changing so don't make assumptions about your agent's fiduciary relationship.

In today's market, most properties are listed on a local computer database called the Multiple Listing Service (or MLS). The seller's broker is responsible for listing the property and managing all subagents and getting the property to a closing table. Many buyers are represented by a buyer's broker who searches the MLS for listed properties. When the buyer has seen the property he likes, his broker will make an offer to the listing broker's office. If the property is not listed by a broker and the buyer is represented by a broker, he can still ask the seller to pay a commission as part of the purchase offer he submits on behalf of his client. Generally, this commission is about 3 percent of the purchase price, but can be negotiated by the parties.

What is a REALTOR?

A REALTOR is a registered-trademark term reserved only for members of the local board of REALTORS, which is affiliated with the National Association of REALTORS. The boards are private, self-regulating agencies that govern rules of conduct for their members. Most brokers belong to one or more local boards; membership is usually a requirement to obtain access to the local Multiple Listing Service (MLS) computer system.

Advantages and Disadvantages of Using a Broker

Let's look at the advantages and disadvantages of using a broker to sell your home.

Cost.   The most obvious issue for the seller is the cost of the commission. The typical real estate commission is 6 percent, which is usually split between the listing broker and the selling broker—that is, the broker who represents and brings the buyer to the table. If your home sells for $300,000 and you owe $250,000, nearly half of your profit will go to commissions. For the buyer, it seems like a no-lose situation, because the seller pays the commission. However, the buyer may effectively be paying a higher price if the sales price is marked up to include the broker's fee. Look at the following three examples:

> Example 1: Stevie Seller has not listed the property with a broker yet. Billy Buyer is interested in buying Stevie Seller's home for $100,000. They consummate the transaction without any brokers, which means that Stevie nets $100,000 and Billy pays $100,000.

> Example 2: Billy wants to use his cousin Bobby Broker to represent him in the transaction. Bobby would require

3 percent of the sales price as a commission. Stevie would only net $97,000 in this case.

Example 3: Stevie Seller meets real estate broker Larry Lister, who takes a listing on the property. He suggests that Stevie list the property for $106,000 to accommodate Larry's 6 percent commission. Bobby Broker brings Billy Buyer to the table with an offer of $106,000. The 6 percent commission amounts to $6,360. Stevie still nets almost $100,000, but Billy paid $6,000 more for the property, than if he had dealt directly with Stevie without any brokers involved.

As you can see from these examples, the cost of the broker's commission usually is paid by the seller's proceeds, but affects either the buyer's total price or the seller's net price.

Sales Price.   While it appears that the seller's proceeds will always be affected negatively by the broker's commission, statistics do show that the sales price of a house is generally higher when a seller uses a real estate broker than when a seller goes the "For Sale by Owner" (FSBO) route. This is partly because the broker can expose the property to more buyers on the MLS. More potential buyers mean more demand, thus more and higher offers. The increased sales price also can be a result of the broker's experience, connections, and skills that allow for better marketing and better negotiating and handling of the sale of the property.

Experience.   The key here is to find the broker with the most successful closed transactions that you can find. There is no substitute for experience. This is the first and most important criteria when deciding whether or not to hire a broker.

Hiring a broker with experience in listing and selling homes and with good selling skills is worth every dime. But don't hire a broker just because she says she has interested buyers. Many real estate brokers suggest to sellers that they have buyers lined up with offers waiting in order to get the seller to list his property. In some cases, a broker will know of potential buyers who may be interested in your house. If that's the case, the broker can represent the buyer in a buyer's agency (see discussion below) and submit an offer on his behalf, saving you 50 percent on the commission.

Time. One of the major reasons you would hire a broker is to save you the time and aggravation of having to show the property, hold open houses, and so forth. If you're not living in the property and have a full-time job, a real estate broker will be worth his weight in gold in terms of time saved. On the other hand, you need to make sure the broker will hustle and get things done. Not every broker who lists does the necessary work to get a property sold. Don't be fooled by a broker who works in an office with 100 other agents; each broker is an independent agent. You want to hire a broker who has almost 24/7 coverage, such as several assistants or a husband-and-wife team. The listing broker's most important function is to make sure that the property gets proper exposure, especially to the other agents.

Help with the Transaction. In most parts of the country, real estate brokers write up the contracts and represent the parties through the closing process. This can be advantageous if you have no idea how to draft a contract. However, there is an economical and more effective option—using a lawyer to represent you. A competent real estate lawyer will charge you about 1 percent or less of the purchase price to draft a contract and deal with all of the legal issues that arise. On a $250,000 house, 1 percent is just $2,500 compared with a 3 percent listing broker commission of $7,500. In most cases, you'll get better representation from a lawyer than a broker when it comes to transactional issues.

To sum it up, you should hire a broker if you're convinced the broker will do the following:

1. Spend sufficient time marketing and managing the sale of your property
2. Get it sold quickly by pricing it right and showing it to a ready list of buyers
3. Take care of all the details of handling the paperwork and closing

Alternatively, you should sell it FSBO (for sale by owner) if

1. You're living in the house and/or have the time to show it
2. You feel confident dealing with the details of the transaction (or can hire an attorney)

3. You can spend time and money aggressively marketing the property

4. You can get the property on the MLS with a discount brokerage agreement

You might try doing both—that is, try selling your house for a few weeks on your own, then list with a broker. If you do list with a broker, make sure you exclude from the listing agreement (in writing) anyone to whom you have shown the property before it was listed. Believe it or not, a listing agreement will generally require that you pay the broker a commission even if you procure the buyer. Although you can technically negotiate this provision out of the listing agreement, most real estate brokers will not permit it for the entire length of the listing agreement. Typically a two-to-three-week partial exclusion is acceptable. In short, read the listing agreement carefully before you sign.

Limited Service or Discount-Fee Brokers

The growing trend is for sellers to use discount-fee brokers, that is, brokers who charge less and offer fewer services. Instead of paying a percentage of the selling price, you pay a smaller flat fee up front, whether or not the house sells. The primary reason for using a discount-fee broker is to gain access to the MLS for your property listing. Since you can't get your property on the MLS without a listing broker, many brokers now offer flat-fee arrangements wherein you pay $500 or less up front and get the house listed on the MLS. The buyer's agent will contact you directly for showings, offers, and so forth. You still have to pay the buyer's agent his commission, which is usually 3 percent of the sales price.

In choosing a discount-service broker, ask the following questions:

- What do I get for the money?
- Which MLS will my house be listed on?
- How quickly will my listing show up on the MLS?
- Can I review the listing by fax before and after it goes live?
- How quickly can your office respond if I want to make changes to the listing?

- How will people contact me for a showing from the listing?
- Does your office offer a showing service for a flat fee?

Remember, you get what you pay for when it comes to service and results with a real estate broker, so consider this choice carefully.

Partial Service, Discounted Fee Approach

There's a growing trend across the country to use the best local full-service broker in their market area at a discounted fee. The idea is to get all the knowledge and experience of the local broker, yet do all the legwork yourself. These duties would include running the open house and re-shows, appointments and any necessary couriering of documents, papers, keys, flyers, and so forth. This time-consuming, non-expertise work is one of the broker's biggest overhead costs. If you were willing to partner up with the top agent, it would be worth your effort. The person known as the facilitator, who is nothing more than your best top broker at a discount, will handle the other elements of the transaction, including advising you on local anomalies and strategies that only seasoned veterans know how to capitalize on. For example, emerging trends and desires of buyers as a whole based on the open house feedback sheets (discussed in Chapter 8) can provide valuable clues as to how and where to outdo the competition.

There's no substitute for frequent experience of negotiating real estate transactions through the voice of an emotionally detached third party. One of the most costly mistakes sellers make is that they get nervous negotiating a big-ticket item, speak too quickly, and unintentionally spoil what would otherwise be a simple transaction. Overcoming the objections of the buyers is best served by a third party who can point out personal experiences of many other transactions she has personally handled. The facilitator's fees depend on how long it takes to get the property sold. A 50 percent discount is typical, provided the transaction completes within a reasonable amount of time.

Will the Real Top Agent Please Stand Up?

Once you've exhausted the option of trying to sell on your own and decided a discount broker is not for you, then it's time to pull out all the stops and find the *best* real estate broker money can buy. All real estate brokers are not created equal. The value in hiring a broker is a direct relationship with the experience and transactions she has successfully completed of homes similar to yours within your defined geography. In other words, you'd want to hire the broker who has most recently and most successfully sold homes in your area within a bracketed price range of your property. The benefits here are threefold.

First, her approach to marketing your house will be based on real-life experiences that have occurred in your current market. Second, you won't waste time guessing whether or not your broker has what it takes to get the property sold for the highest possible price, since she has already proven this with sales and listings similar to your property.

Third, this individual should have a list of fresh buyers ready, able, and willing to buy your property—buyers that are left over from the prior marketing efforts they have exhausted on other properties like yours. For example, just imagine all the advertising dollars and screening of customers that go into any transaction. You, as the seller, can reap the benefits of this past work and save countless hours of wasted time trying to develop a new list of active buyers in the marketplace, but the broker must have already done this with the other properties. We can't emphasize enough the value of this information, provided that the broker has *in fact* successfully completed transactions that can be proved from our original comp book that we developed in Chapter 2. This is where we can separate the successful brokers from the amateurs.

To Tell The Truth

Once upon a time, there was a television show called, *To Tell the Truth*. It consisted of three contestants. All three people were unknown to the general public, yet one person was a highly prominent person in his field, such as a Nobel Peace Prize winner of sorts. The idea of the game was to ask each person questions in such a manner as to root out the actual achiever, while unveiling the imposters. Choosing a top real estate broker is much the same process, if you know the right questions to ask.

The tendency of most real estate brokers is to give you the giggle price as the bottom line, because they know regardless of their talent the seller will usually list with the broker who tells them the highest price for the value of their home. Since the idea is to get the *real* value of what the house should sell for, the antidote for this puffery is the following.

First, narrow down your search to the top three most experienced agents or brokers. Then, tell each broker you are interviewing that you've recently had an independent appraisal of the property and you will hire the broker who gives an opinion of value closest to this appraisal. The fact is that appraisal may not be the most accurate opinion of value, but you're trying to get a broker who knows the market the best and is probably your best candidate to get the property sold, and, more importantly, to get the broker's most *honest* opinion of your property. Keep in mind that the accuracy and timeliness of the broker's response to your request should be equally considered. A truly experienced and honest broker should know almost on the spot what your house should be listed for. However, many of them are reluctant just to give you a number before they've had a chance to give you their sales pitch for listing the property. If you have done your due diligence, you will already know that any of these three brokers would probably do the job just fine. The next most important factor, and perhaps the one that will cause you the least amount of grief, is to hire the broker you like and trust. Since the process of getting a house sold has recently become a matter of months, not weeks, compatibility of personalities can make or break a transaction. It's not just a mere matter of whether the broker will get the job done, but rather whether you can count on her in the hour when she is most needed. Specifically, the broker must be available on the days the negotiations should occur.

One last point worth noting is the backup and support team of the broker you are considering. Everyone needs a day off and a vacation, but you want to make sure your deal is covered no matter what. Husband-and-wife teams tend to be a good choice for this reason. If your broker has several personal assistants, as opposed to office secretaries, this can greatly impact the effectiveness of the transaction.

The Russian Roulette of Real Estate Offices

Since you'll want to know who the best agent is in any office, it may be important to note here how the typical office operates. If you call the main number and ask for representation, you will typically get the next person in line, whomever that may be—the good, the bad, or the ugly. As Forrest Gump said, "Life is like a box of chocolates . . . you never know what you are going to get."

Instead, use your comp book as a guide. If your comp book has just the selling office and not the particular broker, try the Internet (www.toplocalbroker.com).

Commission Sharing

Before you sign on the dotted line on the listing agreement, it's helpful to know what the office policy is about buyer inquiries on your property. Some offices will evenly distribute the calls of interest on your property to the next available selling agent in the office, regardless of who the listing broker is in the office. The reason for this is that the office needs to feed all of the agents to keep them working in the office. The horrifying implication for the seller is that the incentive for the listing broker is diluted because another agent is sharing equally in the fee. And the worst problem of this list is that the listing broker is the one who bears the greatest amount of expense in getting the property sold. Make sure your top broker is working under an office whose policy is to direct all inquiries directly to him or his personal assistants.

Who's on Call?

Whoever answers the phone rocks the cradle. Is it any random agent, rotation order, secretary, assistant, janitor, answering machine, or answering service? What is the response time? Is the agent's cell phone readily given out? Does the office procedure allow easy access to making appointments and showing the property? Discuss with your broker the office policy about sharing keys with other offices if they don't use lockboxes.

You Get What You Pay For

Until recently, the broker fee structures have varied greatly from the familiar 6 percent.

The old adage of "you get what you pay for" applies here, assuming you're hiring a top agent. Obviously, not all agents are top agents, but the same office will charge the same fee regardless of which agent you end up with. Office-to-office fee structures can also vary. The bottom line here is that often the fee is not the greatest expense in the transaction. It's the lack of achieving the highest possible price within the least amount of time that usually ends up being the largest cost to the property owner. As counterintuitive as it may seem, offering a higher fee to the selling agent than your competitors will often yield a higher selling price because of the greater attention your property will receive. One crucial thing to know here is what the selling agent is getting paid. Fee-structure splits among agents are not widely known. Though it does vary from state to state, and from market condition to market condition, the same basic principle will apply. Some states require dual agency when the listing agent is also the selling agent of the same firm. Make sure and get an explanation of your agent as to the legal relationship you may now have from them as a result. Dual agency is when the same firm represents both the seller and the buyer on the same transaction.

There are two sides to every fee, the listing side and the selling side. Make sure the selling broker's part of the fee is the part that should be higher than the compensation paid to selling brokers by your competitors. If your neighbor is selling a house that's just like yours, find out what the selling broker is getting as compensation, and outdo it by just a little. Studies have shown that a slightly higher amount will gain the favor of the selling brokers. If the neighbors are listed for a 5 percent gross-listing fee, and their listing broker is offering 2 percent selling broker's compensation, then the incentive you offer should be between 2.25 percent and 2.5 percent. The gross fee or commission paid is all a seller will typically pay for the transaction. However, few sellers or their listing brokers discuss or review what the selling agents are being offered for compensation. In a soft market, the higher the compensation you give to the selling agent—as compared to the other sellers' offerings—the greater the advantage that your listing will have. We know of many brokers who prioritize the homes with higher fees for them. The brokers will ultimately show all the listings that would meet their buyer's criteria, but they may bump some to the back of the line. Lastly, remember that brokerage fees are almost always negotiable, especially if the full asking price has not been met. The broker's fee is automatically reduced when the selling price is reduced, since the fee is a percentage amount of the selling price and not the listing price.

The Function of the Listing Broker

There is a major misconception in the industry—when they hire a listing agent, sellers often believe that this agent is the one to sell their house. This couldn't be further from the truth. Although a broken clock is right twice a day, and it is not uncommon for the listing agent to sell the house herself, it should not be the focus of the listing agent to concentrate on anything else than the following items:

1. Insure that the property photos are as flattering as possible

2. Insure that the information in the listing is accurate and complete

3. Insure that the property has the full exposure to all agents in the marketplace

4. Insure that the property is properly positioned pricewise against the competition

5. Insure that a regular review of the property's showing activity and follow up calls made by all interested parties

Just as an orchestra conductor is there to keep the musicians in harmony and lead the group, a listing broker's function is there to coordinate and maintain an orderly process among the customers and the selling agents. This becomes enormously beneficial when more than one party is interested in the property. The listing agent can act as a referee and attempt to elicit the highest and best offer from each of the interested parties, while maintaining a relatively objective position. Remember, regardless of which agent sells the property, the listing agent will still collect her fee. Listing brokers often have a difficult time handling selling agents since only one selling agent can prevail in selling the property, while the other may be disgruntled.

Some agents can't negotiate since it is ultimately the policy of the brokerage office in most cases that dictate the fee structure. Top agents are given the leeway to negotiate fees as they deem appropriate under the circumstances. Low market activity and long days-on-market areas tend to create environments where broker profits are greatly diminished. Many brokers end up going broke. Choosing to interview solid brokerage operations can be very important. A well-known discount-fee franchise operation on the East Coast recently filed for bankruptcy since the inherent business model could not survive in a slow market. Don't try to reinvent the wheel here. Go back and check your agent's expertise, experience, and years in the business as well as the number of closed transactions. If you have a good friend in the business, it would be wise to review the comp book with that person before setting up your interviews with brokers.

Measure Twice, Cut Once

Review your listing before it goes on the MLS. You only get one chance to make a good first impression. Before the information, photos, and descriptions of your property are launched into the market, sit down with your agent, and review what is going to appear to the public and other brokers. Too many times we have seen listings entered that have no picture or description. The process of elimination is practiced by both the buyers and the active selling agents (as opposed to listing agents) in the market. They'll quickly judge whether or not to make an appointment to see your property or just let it languish. Amazingly as it may seem, this part of the process is one of the things that separates the people who get their houses sold quickly from the ones who end up trying for months with no avail. The key difference is that buyers tend to make snap judgments and ignore a house, after they've formed an unfavorable opinion of it based on a first impression. This is exponentially true as the number of homes accumulate on the market.

Before pressing the button to list your house, compare your listing one last time to the others for sale and to the ones sold. This one last comparison may be worth thousands. Focus on the highest-valued items for comparison sake first. That curb-appeal photo would certainly get most of our attention. If you have your done comp-book homework, the work of the listing agents is before you. The selling agents are often better at selling than checking the detail work of a listing that nowadays seems to be broadcasted to many other sights after its initial listing onto the local MLS. Should you decide to list with a top selling agent, as opposed to a top listing agent, then the initial review of the listing information is that much more important. On the other hand, should you list with a top listing agent, more review will be needed in the follow-up with the buyers department. Both types of top agents have their advantages and disadvantages. Trust and gut instinct can help you decide between the two. Most importantly, your ability to update and modify your listing based on feedback is always an option.

If you have an independent third-party expert, then use that person. Almost everyone knows a few real estate agents. Some may even be family members. Listing with them should only be considered, in our opinion, if they meet the criteria for the top local broker. Assuming that this is not the case, then it is a big help to have an insider keeping an eye on the progress of your broker. Keep in mind that the broker you have chosen will have the greatest knowledge of the local marketing strategies. However, once you are listed your friend in the business can check on the listing quality as compared to the market as it evolves. Most MLS systems have a public access site that you can check for yourself.

Try acting as a buyer and search for your own home. This may reveal some interesting search parameters that you may not have considered when listing the property. That would be a good time to call your broker and modify your listing to fall within as many category searches as possible that buyers might try.

Timing Is Everything

Make sure your listing hits market at the best possible time. It's imperative that the listing enters the pool at just the right time. Most buyers and real estate professionals have set up and committed to their schedule before Friday afternoon. So the best time to get in front of the marketplace would be clearly before that time.

Studies have shown that listings entered on weekends or the earlier part of the week tend to get lost in the shuffle. The less obvious reasons for this are that most brokers and agents work with buyers on the weekends and take off a few days during the week, typically Tuesday, Wednesday, or Thursday. To achieve the highest level of critical first-day-on-the-market exposure, it's best in our opinion to get onto any listing service on a Thursday or, preferably, before 9 A.M. Friday. We've tested various days and times that the same listing was entered and have received widely different results. Entering the listing on a Monday was the worst day, since most buyers and brokers are focused on negotiating offers they have received over the weekend and tend to pay the least amount of attention to new listings since they are not ready to go out looking again. Who has ever bought a home without first seeing the inside? Nine-tenths of end-user buyers are going to look over the weekends and confirm their appointments to see these homes no later than lunchtime on Friday.

The effectiveness of timing can't be underestimated. It's not just the timing of the weekday; it's also the timing of the weekend. Holiday weekends are notorious for very low-volume buyer turnouts, whether it's for showings or open houses. In either case, attendance is typically 50 percent or less than on a weekend that does not include a holiday. Let's not forget that major media and sports events can have the same influence as major holidays. Having said this, real estate sellers can take advantage of this fact by using the pent-up demand to increase their initial exposure on the market. For example, putting your listing on the market at 8 A.M. on the Friday of the weekend following the Super Bowl should have three times the attention and exposure of a listing entered on Super Bowl weekend itself. Labor Day, Memorial Day, and the Fourth of July weekends are all taboo for launching your initial exposure to the market. Seasonal timing is also important to the overall effectiveness of the sales process. It would be interesting to note the actual contract dates, as opposed to the closing dates of the sales in your comp book. These clues may give you inside information as to the anomalies of timing in your specific geographic area. Generally speaking, between Thanksgiving Day and New Year's Day is the worst time of the year to launch your listing on to the marketplace, because the least number of buyers are paying attention during this time period. Common sense would dictate that spring will yield the most buyers during the year. Competitive supply is also proportionately higher as well. All things being equal, January supply compared to demand is lower and often exploited by seasoned investors who have discovered this by accident over decades of trial and error. Lastly, it is the comp book and its clues that will often open up marketing strategies like the specific timing for your specific market.

Initial exposure that is well done, versus poorly planned, can not only make the difference between getting the house sold or not, but also the difference between a low and high offer from a buyer who feels the competitive (or lackluster) environment of an open house. Studies have shown that the initial exposure to the market is one of the most important parts of the entire sales process. We have concluded that this simple distinction of proper timing can account for one of the greatest influences a seller or broker can have on achieving the highest price for the property. It's when the property first goes on the market that it receives the greatest amount of attention. Making this work for you is the greatest tool you have available at no cost!

If you've already listed your property during a slow time, there are some corrective remedies. There's nothing preventing an owner from relisting a property, or what insiders call the "re-bake." Re-baking is taking a stale listing off the market, waiting a weekend or two and then re-listing the property with a new picture from a new angle at a somewhat more aggressive listing price. The difference may not be as obvious as it seems—it's not just about reducing the price, since price reductions are often the least noted activities on the multiple-listing reports. It's the new listing on the market that gets the attention, much like a headline in a newspaper. Literally, the price and other changes are often so far down the list of market activity reports that buyers and brokers are rarely able to take in all the information that occurs in a marketplace. For example, on a Monday, for the average-sized active market, there may be hundreds of changes that occur, compared to perhaps only a handful of new listings.

Some Realtor boards prevent re-baked listings. If this is the case, give your real estate broker several listings on your property with varying expiration times. Thus, instead of a six-month listing, give your broker three two-month listings. Most listing services cannot stop you from employing this strategy. The advantage is obviously to enhance your initial exposure. What's not obvious is the degree of vicarious exposure through new-listing focus.

Broader Strokes of Data Entry: An Art Worth a Few Percentage Points in Your Favor

Studies have shown that the ultimate selling price of the house is a function of the number of people that see it. The number of people who see it is a result of interest generated. To generate the greatest number of hits of interest on your property, think in terms of entering your features with the broadest strokes possible. Most MLS and other listing services have specific questions to answer concerning your featured amenities. Consider the basic seven- or eight-room colonial-style home with two full baths, three bedrooms, and a family room on the first floor. It would make a significant difference in most market areas by entering the family room as also a possible bedroom for a parent or relative unable to climb the stairs. Even if this family room needs a minor conversion like a door and a closet to make it an official bedroom, advertise and market it as if it were. Simply offer the buyer a credit at closing for the conversion, if they want it as a bedroom.

The idea here is to get as many possible hits of interest in the property by accommodating as many family needs as possible. Furthermore, studies have shown that in the case of the two-bedroom house, selling prices tend to be significantly higher for a three-bedroom version of the same home. If at all possible, simply offer the buyers a credit for perhaps a family-room conversion to a third bedroom. In the case of room conversions outside of the current living space, such as with attics or garage conversions, make sure and check with your local municipalities for their regulations and laws. Local building inspectors and not their staff are the ones to consult with. This person is usually an architect or an engineer hired by the governing body. *Do not* just represent that these conversions can be done; check it out. Legal usage and representations of the property's habitability can be crucial. These are usually dictated in the Certificate of Occupancy, Certificate of Compliance, or Certificate of Completion (depending on local lingo). When in doubt, check it out!

Make sure to have a once-over check with either yourself or your broker, again before launching into the market. Omissions of key data are also very critical, since we now live in an e-mail, automated-response world. A very good example of this would be to omit key data simply due to lack of knowledge. Don't think that entering this information later is a substitute for effective initial exposure value. For example, elderly couples and brokers unfamiliar with an area tend to forget or not know the school district numbers or names. Be warned that this is one of the most commonly neglected items by amateurs. The consequences of this are latent in nature. Since schools are top-of-the-list criteria for most buyers, they will enter searches with a school district in mind. If the school district information is omitted or incorrect, it will not come up correctly in a search for this criterion. Conversely, certain MLS systems allow you to use such data in your favor. For example, if your property is in the Shady Acres subdivision and the adjacent subdivision is named Shady Estates, simply entering Shady as the subdivision or listing *both* Shady Acres and Shady Estates as the subdivision will bring up your listing on searches for houses in either subdivision.

This brings up another key point. If you live in an area with a special name, make sure to use it to give yourself a distinction from your competitors. For example, on many deeds, there once was a builder who divided up an existing parcel and that parcel had a nice name to it, such as the Silver Stocking district of the Gibson section of Valley Stream, New York. What makes this so nice is that it gives you the ability to tell the story of origin. Romancing the history of your area can certainly give chills to the buyer. It is largely an emotional purchase and capitalizing on this through the story of how it all began can really make the emotional difference, especially if the buyer is looking at another home in the same general area. You can separate yourself by the distinction of location, which as we all know is what it's all about. One of our favorite closing statements regarding this situation is to end with, "Well you know the three most important things about real estate right—location, location, location!"

Who could argue with that?

Chapter Summary

- Try selling the property on your own first.
- Learn how to flush out the best brokers in your area.
- Due your due diligence on a broker.
- Make sure your listing is entered into the MLS correctly.

CHAPTER 7

Owner Financing—
Your Secret Weapon
in a Soft Market

If you doubt money has value, go try and borrow some.
                                        —Benjamin Franklin

To sell a house quickly, it must be attractive and so should the terms. By fixing your home to present it in the best light and offering flexible terms as well, you have in fact made your buyer an offer he can't refuse. When offering your house for an all-cash purchase only, you limit your market. If you're flexible on the financing terms of the property, you increase your pool of buyers and thus the demand for your house. Take your guidance from retailers such as Best Buy and Circuit City, companies that offer attractive financing to sell computers and appliances. The more attractive the terms, the more people will want to buy, simply because they have no other way to purchase a home. Strategies such as owner financing or selling on a lease-option agreement are ways that will help you to sell your home for top dollar, and, in most cases, allow you to receive positive monthly cash flow.

If you're in a particularly tough market and don't have a lot of leeway to drop your price, consider offering owner-financing terms to attract more buyers. Owner financing makes it easier to move a house, because it will attract more buyers without traditional bank financing.

An owner-financed transaction is one in which the seller accepts anything less than all cash at closing. Let's step back and define an all-cash closing. An all-cash closing doesn't necessarily mean the buyer walks into closing with a briefcase full of money—"all cash" means the seller *gets* certified funds (actually, the seller may use most of the cash to pay off the existing mortgage loan, so she walks away with *some* proceeds). If the seller accepts any part of the purchase price in the form of payments after the closing date, then it's an owner-carry sale. An owner-carry sale may require the seller to finance, or carry, all or part of the entire purchase price.

Advantages of Owner Financing

There are many advantages of owner financing over conventional financing for the buyer and seller. It's important for you to understand these concepts so you can explain and sell it to your potential buyer.

Easy Qualification

If you browse through the newspaper on a weekend, you will see dozens of advertisements for cars, furniture, electronics, and other consumer products with the words "pay later" or "special financing" prominently displayed. The world of consumer goods is credit driven, and it's a proven fact that attractive financing terms will sell any product faster than all cash.

Owner financing on houses is more attractive than conventional financing, because it doesn't require a traditional lender's income-and-credit approval. If your buyer has poor credit or no provable income, the traditional route of institutional financing may not work. With the collapse of the subprime market, fewer lenders offer low, fixed-interest-rate loans to people with poor credit. The last thing you want is to sell a house and then have the deal fall through before closing because the buyer's financial qualifications didn't meet his lender's loan criteria. Or, more likely, owner financing may be used as a back-up plan if the buyer is unable to qualify for his loan, but is still interested in purchasing your house.

If your buyer is an investor, lenders may be leery about extending too much credit to him if he owns multiple properties. When an investor does own a number of properties, he may not be able to qualify for the best loan programs that offer the lowest interest rates. It makes sense for investors to save their credit and only borrow from traditional sources when absolutely necessary. Thus by offering owner financing to investors, you open up a new pool of potential buyers, creating more demand and a quicker sale.

Cheaper Closing Costs

One of the biggest benefits for the buyer can be avoiding the costs associated with conventional loans. Points, origination fees, underwriting charges, appraisal, credit reports and a plethora of other junk fees charged by conventional lenders can amount to thousands of dollars at closing. An owner-financed transaction eliminates most of these costs, allowing the seller to get more cash in his pocket, or, if the buyer does not have money for such costs, to attract more potential buyers who can only put down scant cash to close.

Faster Closing

An owner-financed transaction can close in a matter of days. By skirting lender approval, survey, appraisal, and other delay factors, you can go from contract to close much faster. A closing can be done by a title company, escrow company, or attorney, which can be accomplished within a week. A traditional closing can take weeks or months if any of the ancillary parties (appraiser, inspector, and so forth) drag their feet.

A Workaround for Down Payment Requirements

Selling with owner financing is a nice short-term strategy to work around lender down-payment requirements for the buyer. For purchase-money loans, lending guidelines require a certain down payment by the borrower. For refinance loans, however, the guidelines are strictly based on a loan-to-value (LTV) formula.

For example, let's say Salina Seller has a property worth $100,000 that she agrees to sell to Bunny Buyer for $80,000. Lending guidelines for ABC Savings Bank state that the loan may not exceed an 80 percent loan-to-value (LTV) ratio. So, in theory, Bunny could borrow $80,000—the entire purchase price. However, ABC's lending guidelines limit the loan to 80 percent of the purchase price or appraisal, *whichever is less*. Thus, Bunny needs to put $16,000 down (or 20 percent of $80,000) and ABC will lend her $64,000 (80 percent of $80,000). Furthermore, Bunny will probably pay about $5,000 in costs to get the loan from ABC.

If Salina sells her property to Bunny for $80,000 with owner financing terms and little or no money down, six months later Bunny could refinance the existing loan without having to take money out of her pocket. Lenders typically require 6 to 12 months of "seasoning" (ownership) on a property before they'll lend based on the appraised value versus the lower purchase price. The refinance loan guidelines for ABC Savings Bank are an 80 percent LTV for Bunny's credit and income qualifications. Because Bunny has owned the property for six months, ABC will offer a refinance loan based on 80 percent of the property's *appraised* value, which is $80,000 (80 percent × $100,000) under this scenario. The $80,000 would be used to pay off the balance of the owner-financed loan to Salina. So, in the long run, Bunny loses less out-of-pocket cash and is able to purchase the home immediately from Salina, which also solves her dilemma. Seasoning requirements tend to change from time to time, so check current requirements from lenders.

Owner Financing Mechanics

Let's discuss the mechanics of the owner financing, which is different if the seller has existing financing on the property.

Property Owned Free and Clear

Let's begin with a simple explanation of owner financing for a property that is owned free and clear of any mortgage liens; that is, there is no debt owed on the property. Let's say Sally Seller owns her home free and clear—that is, she owes nothing to the bank and there are no mortgage liens on the property. Sally agrees to sell her property to Barney Buyer for $100,000, with the terms of 5 percent down and owner-financing for $95,000 (95 percent of the purchase price). At closing, Barney tenders $5,000 in cash and signs an IOU (known as a "promissory note") for $95,000. Sally executes and delivers a deed (ownership of the property) to Barney. The promissory note is secured by a mortgage that is recorded against the property as a lien in favor of Sally. In this case, Sally is essentially acting as a lender to fund part of the purchase price of the house.

Sally can set a balloon date in the promissory note by which the loan has to be paid in full, at which time Barney must either sell the property or get a new loan from a traditional source such as a bank or mortgage lender. When the new loan is obtained, the loan to Sally is paid off, and the mortgage lien is removed from the property. In some states a different form of mortgage called a "deed of trust" is used. A state-by-state list can be found in the resource directory in Appendix I.

Seller Has a Mortgage, But Some Equity

The preceding example is for illustrative purposes only, because if you're reading this manual you probably owe money to a lender secured by a mortgage lien on your property. Let's consider a more common example—a house that has some equity because it has appreciated since it was purchased, or was purchased with a sizeable down payment.

Let's say Sammy Seller owns a property worth $100,000 that's encumbered by a mortgage of $80,000. Sammy agrees to sell the property to Betty Buyer for $100,000. Because there's $20,000 in equity ($100,000 value minus the $80,000 loan), Betty offers to pay $10,000 down and borrow the balance of the $90,000 from Manny Mortgage Lender. At the last minute before closing, Manny decides that Betty Buyer's eyes are the wrong color and refuses to fund her loan. Instead, Manny offers to lend $80,000, which is $10,000 short of the amount Betty needs to close. One choice is for Sammy to drop the price of $90,000. Another choice is for Sammy and Betty to part ways and for Sammy to put the property back on the market to find another buyer.

A third choice is for Sammy to accept a promissory note for $10,000 as part of the purchase price. At closing, Betty will pay Sammy $10,000 down, borrow $80,000 from Manny and give Sammy a promissory note for $10,000. Sammy signs over to Betty a deed to the property, and Betty signs a mortgage lien for $80,000 to Manny, who will possess a first lien on the property. Betty also signs another mortgage lien to Sammy, who will have a second mortgage on the property. In a year or so, Betty gets a new loan for $90,000, paying off both the first (Manny's) and second (Sammy's) mortgage liens. In the meantime, Betty can make Sammy payments of interest on the $10,000 promissory note, which is a nice income stream for Sammy.

Seller Has a Mortgage, and Little or No Equity

If the seller has little or no equity but a reasonably low payment on his note (whether a fixed-rate loan or fixed for a few more years), he can sell the property by using a wraparound transaction. A "wraparound" or "wrap," is an arrangement wherein you sell a property encumbered with existing financing by accepting payments in monthly installments, leaving the existing loan in place. The seller uses the payments he collects from the buyer to continue making payments on the underlying mortgage note.

For example, Susie Seller owns a house worth $100,000 and she owes $90,000 to First Federal Financial on a favorable 6 percent, 30-year, fixed-rate loan. Her principal and interest payments on the loan are roughly $600 per month. She can sell the property for $100,000 for cash, but this might take a few months and $6,000 or more in broker fees and concessions, leaving breadcrumbs on the table after Susie pays off her loan. Susie advertises the property as for sale by owner (FSBO) with owner financing and sells the property to Barry Buyer for $100,000, taking $5,000 down and carrying the balance of $95,000 at 8 percent for 30 years. Susie doesn't pay off her underlying loan, but rather collects payments from Barry (roughly $700 per month) and continues to make payments on the underlying loan (roughly $600 per month). Susie collects $100 per month cash flow on the "spread" until Barney refinances.

Mechanics of a Wraparound Transaction

A wraparound is commonly done with an installment land contract. The installment land contract is an agreement by which the buyer makes payments to the seller under an agreement of sale. The transaction is also known by the expressions "contract for deed" or "agreement for deed." The seller holds title as collateral until the balance is paid. In many ways, the installment land contract is similar to a mortgage, in that the buyer takes possession of the property, maintains it, and pays taxes and insurance. However, the deed remains in the seller's name until the balance of the debt is paid by the buyer.

An installment land contract usually contains a forfeiture provision, under which a defaulting buyer may be evicted like a defaulting tenant. Under the contract, legal title remains in the seller's name until the purchase price is satisfied. When the buyer satisfies the indebtedness, legal title passes to the buyer.

Advertising for an Owner-Financing Buyer

Advertising for an owner-financing buyer should be substantially similar to advertising for a cash deal except that you should be able find a buyer who's not represented by a broker. Since you're taking substantially less cash as down payment and carrying most of the financing, there's less available to pay a broker fee. Thus, you should use yard signs, flyers, web sites and possibly an ad in the rentals section of your local newspaper. The reason for advertising in the rental section is to attract people who might otherwise be looking for a rental, not knowing that easy qualification for owner financing is available.

Modest, vinyl signs strategically placed at major intersections within a one-mile radius of the property can bring a flood of potential buyers. The key words on the sign are No Credit Required—Owner Will Finance. Remember, it's important that you do a thorough background check on any possible buyer. The last thing you want is a buyer who fails to make his payments, so screen a buyer the same as you would any tenant. National Tenant Network (www.ntnonline.com) is a good resource for doing background checks. Finally, although they don't need credit or qualifications to obtain a loan at this time, they will need to refinance and pay you off within the balloon period, which is generally about 24 months. You shouldn't sell to a buyer with owner financing who has a slim chance of getting a loan to cash you out within 24 months.

The Lease/Option—Cousin to Owner Financing

A lease/option is another alternative to a cash sale. With interest rates rising and guidelines for subprime mortgages tightening, demand for rental properties has increased. Likewise, demand for alternative financing arrangements such as owner financing and lease/options has followed suit. The lease/option is an excellent way to move a property quickly in a slow real estate market with steady demand for rentals.

What Is a Lease/Option?

A lease/option is actually a combination of two transactions; (1) a lease agreement and (2) a purchase option. The purchase option generally runs concurrent with the lease agreement.

An *option* is a unilateral or one-way agreement. Like a regular purchase agreement, the seller is bound to sell the property to the buyer at an agreed-upon price. However, the buyer has the option to complete the purchase or not complete the purchase, at his choice. The buyer (known as the optionee) generally gives the seller (the optionor) a nonrefundable payment for the purchase option, which is typically 2 percent to 3 percent of the purchase price. The lease agreement provides that the buyer is responsible for repairs and maintenance during the term of the agreement.

Advantages of a Lease/Option for the Seller

The main advantage of the lease/option for the seller is that he gets the property occupied quickly, with the lease payments covering most or all of his monthly mortgage payment. The deal can be consummated quickly, without the need of waiting for third-party lender financing to consummate the agreement. For-rent-by-owner web sites (www.rentals.com) make it cheap, fast, and easy to find a buyer for a lease/option transaction.

Disadvantages of a Lease/Option for the Seller

The main disadvantage of using a lease/option is that on higher-priced homes, the rental payment won't cover the underlying monthly payment. Thus a $400,000 house may only rent for $2,000 a month with a mortgage payment of $3,000 a month. In addition, the seller/owner continues to pay for taxes and insurance. A work-around for this problem is to refinance the property with an interest-only payment or adjustable-rate mortgage that's fixed for two or more years. Even so, the monthly spread could still be negative, but having a $300-a-month negative cash flow is better for most sellers than a $3,000-a-month negative cash flow, as in the case of a vacant property. The goal in this case would be to get the tenant/buyer qualified as soon as possible for a mortgage loan to complete the purchase of the property. This requires some knowledge of how to improve one's credit, which can be done with the assistance of a mortgage broker.

Advantages of a Lease/Option for the Buyer

For the buyer, the lease/option is a great way to get into a home with a low down payment. Also, since the buyer isn't required to complete the purchase; it's a good way to try before you buy. The buyer also may have credit challenges or a recent bankruptcy that he needs time to overcome, before qualifying for bank financing. As with an owner-financed deal, you shouldn't sell to a tenant/buyer who has little or no chance of getting a loan to cash you out within 24 months.

Disadvantages of a Lease/Option for the Buyer

The disadvantage for the buyer is that his option payment isn't refundable if he doesn't complete the purchase of the home. Also, the price he'll pay is generally not discounted, because the buyer doesn't have the same purchasing power as someone who can qualify for a loan and buy the house outright. Furthermore, the lease/option doesn't give the buyer the tax advantages of ownership until the option is exercised and the sale is complete. Thus, the buyer can't deduct his payments for rent each month as he could if he were making interest payments on a land contract.

How to Find Lease/Option Buyers

The best way to find lease/option buyers is to advertise in the rental section of the newspaper and on the Internet (www.rentals.com). Also, a good yard sign and directional signs will generate a lot of calls. The signs and ads should have the headline RENT-TO-OWN to pull the most number of calls. The expression "rent-to-own" is more friendly and familiar to consumers than "lease with option."

Mortgage brokers and real estate brokers can also be a good source of leads. The mortgage broker will get a chance to profit by getting a loan for the tenant/buyer. A real estate broker can get a delayed commission when the buyer exercises his option to buy.

Terms of the Deal

The lease payment should be advertised at basically the same rate as market rent for a similar house, otherwise you'll get fewer calls on the ads. The price will be determined by what the house will appraise for, and it works much better if your house is one of the smaller ones in the neighborhood. So, for example, if the neighborhood values go from $220,000 to $260,000, pricing it in the middle (from $240,000 to $250,000) should work well, even if a qualified cash buyer wouldn't pay more than $220,000 for a cash sale. As long as the price can be justified with an appraisal a year from now, the price is whatever a buyer is willing to pay. As you can see, offering flexible terms for a buyer allows you to charge a greater price.

Getting Your Buyer Qualified for a Loan

Getting your buyer qualified for a loan is the end game with a lease/option, especially if you have negative cash flow and want to take your equity out of the property. The key to getting your tenant/buyer cashed out is helping him get his credit score high enough to qualify for a loan. This involves understanding how credit works and what things will improve it. To help your buyer establish a good credit reporting history, report your payments (to www.rentreporters.com).

Lease/Option Versus Land Contract

A lease/option arrangement is not a sale, but rather a landlord–tenant relationship. The IRS generally treats an installment land contract as a sale, which means the buyer has the tax benefits of ownership. Thus, the payments of interest made by the buyer in possession are deductible as mortgage interest, even though the buyer doesn't have legal title to the property. The lease/option is a landlord-tenant relationship until the purchase is complete, so the seller will claim the property as a rental until such time the tenant/buyer exercises his option to purchase.

Which formula is better? It depends on the situation and your goals. A lease/option transaction isn't a sale, so you benefit from market appreciation if you are in an appreciating market. If you are in a declining market and sell the property for a loss, a lease/option will allow you to take a tax write off as a rental property. Review this with your tax advisor if this is the case.

A land-contract sale allows you to get more of a down payment from the buyer, since it feels more like a sale. In addition, you'll get a higher payment from an owner-financed sale. In highly priced neighborhoods, the rents may not command enough to cover your underlying mortgage payments on a lease/option. A land-contract sale allows you to collect principal and interest payments, which would typically be more than you could collect in rent.

Chapter Summary

- Creative financing can help you move a house in a slow market.
- You can get a higher price with an owner-financed sale or lease/option.

CHAPTER 8

The Right Way to Do
an Open House

ABC—Always Be Closing.
    —Alex Baldwin, from the movie, *Glengarry Glenross*

Now that you're ready to roll, it's time to start marketing and bringing customers to your door. Here's the bottom line: get as many people through your door as possible. While showings are important, the open house will be your most effective tool for getting buyers into your net so you can close them into a deal. This chapter will cover how to get your customers to your open house and how to handle them once they walk through your door. We'll leave the price negotiations part of the sale for Chapter 9.

Preliminary negotiation is the foundation upon which the success of achieving the highest possible price is based. If correctly handled from the beginning, the price goal will happen naturally and will take less effort and stress than one might think. The insider's secret here is that one single objective must be met before any other. Getting the buyers to like and trust you takes time. That's one of the reasons for making the open house a relaxed and pleasant experience. At that time, your goal as the seller, or seller's agent, is to take your time and let the buyers lead the way. The best brokers stay out of the way and let the buyers set the pace of the showing through the home for the first time. We'll cover this later and in detail. For now, simply keep in mind that the goal is to get the buyers to like and trust you and feel that you really care. As the old saying goes, "No one cares how much you know until they know how much you care."

It's a Numbers' Game

As we discussed in Chapter 1, it's all a numbers' game with the buyers. The purpose of marketing is to bring as many people to the house as possible. The more people who view the house, the better chance that you'll get an offer that makes sense. It follows that you'll also have a better chance of closing a deal and cashing a check. Ideally, your marketing efforts will lead to a euphoric state of having two buyers both making offers at the same time. This is a dangerous situation if not handled properly, which we'll cover later in Chapter 9 on negotiations.

Babe Ruth and many top athletic professionals understood this concept better than anyone. It's a matter of how many times you try before you reach your goal. Babe Ruth had a reputation for both a high number of home runs and a commensurately high number of strikeouts. If you don't get up to the plate, you never have a chance to round the bases. This concept translates well to real estate sales. We've found that the proportion of 100:10:1 is a magic ratio. This would mean that it should take about 100 RAW buyers (ready, able, and willing) to bring you 10 who actually look at the property (hopefully during the open house), which will result in the one best and highest bidder. It's so important to realize that this buyer may come at any time. However, most of the time the buyer comes at the beginning; sometimes it's the very first buyer who sees the property. This creates an unfortunate situation for a seller. Sellers often get lulled into a false sense of security by the activity level from the initial launch into the market during the first weeks. If you've not done your due diligence, and we *mean it*, this will be your greatest mistake of all. You must know where the value boundaries of your property fall to know where the bull and bear boundaries lie. Earlier in the book, we called them the giggle and no brainer tests. This distinction deserves a repeated explanation.

The giggle test is the price in which even you know the property is at its highest possible value. The no-brainer test is the value at which you can sell it to any buyer relatively quickly. The middle point is the sweet spot. Working from the sweet spot and using this as your core point will give you the success you need. This is the highest and best selling tool you can have. Having the facts at your finger tips gives you the confidence you'll need to push a deal forward. You'll thank yourself time and time again.

Residential sales in a typical market require your constant reference to the comp book. You want to be the indisputable expert of value based on your ability to specifically reference addresses, names, sales prices, and features of the homes sold and for sale that will enhance your property's value by comparison. For example, we love to mention what the Jones family just paid for a property that was almost identical to the subject property. The subject property is the property that you want to sell. Bank appraisers consider this the property that they'll compare all others to, in their search for the closest like-kind sale.

Knowledge of your property's inherent range value will also let you know which buyers are the most serious. The greatest majority of times, the authentic buyer will make an offer closest to their highest offer. The lowball bidders are often lacking one of the three key elements to be considered among the elite 10 buyers we need to screen out. For example, let's say your asking price is $299,000 and you know from your comp book that the average selling price amongst your successful competitors is in the range of 90 percent to 95 percent of asking price. The real buyer would typically start at an offer of 90 percent of your asking price, which in this case would be about $270,000. If a buyer presents a $250,000 offer, it would be statistically probable to assume this is not the buyer you want to spend time on in negotiations. Based on three decades of experience and thousands of transactions, it is here and now that we would suggest you politely decline the offer. If the offer is less than 90 percent of your asking price, an appropriate response would be a no thank you and ask them to resubmit a higher offer.

Before we get into the intricacies of negotiations, we'll lay the foundation. This will be the setting, the ambience, the right personality, and the proper amount of interaction you should have with your buyer. There is a time and place in which things should be said and done. We'll sketch out the generalities here, but bear in mind there are always exceptions to the rules, especially if you think the buyer is ready to sign. At that point, you can use our simple John Wayne Three-Step Approach that we'll discuss in Chapter 9.

Be Prepared

If you're going to go through the trouble of bringing a lot of people through your house, be prepared for the questions and concerns they may have. Look at the house through the eyes of the buyer. What questions would you ask if you were in their shoes? Your comp book and list of documents we discussed in Chapter 5 will be extremely valuable. Have all the information you need at your fingertips. Questions the buyers may have are some of the same as you had when you bought your property. Here are five things to keep in mind:

1. **Schools.** If you're unprepared to answer the question with all of the pertinent information, your buyer will be distracted as he looks through the home asking, "Does this even fit into my criteria?"

2. **Ancillary Expenses.** Taxes, utility bills, water and sewer, and HOA dues should be ready and available on a flier or separate folder with photocopies only by request. Unless you own a special tax-exemption or fuel-efficient home, don't offer it up without a request. Remember, the big print giveth, and the small print taketh away!

3. **What's Your Story?** The obvious and important question just about every buyer will ask is "Why are you selling?" You need to have the answer to this down pat. You should be sad to give up your beautiful home, no matter what the story behind it. You don't want to say something like, "I am moving to a quieter neighborhood." No matter what, don't complain about your neighbors!

4. **Honesty is always the best policy.** Keep it short and sweet.

5. **Promotional Materials.** Give two flyers to each person who walks into the house, as well as a business-card flier of the home stapled to the top. People who don't like carrying around flyers will place the business card in their wallet and pass it to others.

Go Fish!

Get a fish bowl with index-card sized questionnaires and a photograph of 10 fifty dollar bills on the front for effect. Each visitor to the open house will fill out a card with her information and guess the final sales price of the house. The winner of the raffle who comes closest to the actual selling price wins the $500 prize. The idea is to offer a raffle at the open house to gather names of your potential buyers and get their opinions as to what the highest and lowest possible price this house could sell for. We're trying to implement the same price-range strategy, except from the buyers' eyes. It would be appropriate to offer a $1,000 raffle for a $1 million home or a $250 raffle for a $250,000 house. Just as statisticians can poll a cross-section of a population and determine the aggregate results of a larger population, you can implement the same strategy and reach the same objective. For example, if you obtain 27 opinions of value, you might get a few absurdly high and low estimates, but the average of the balance of consensus of opinion will be close to the actual value that someone will pay. In addition, you will quickly ascertain the inexperienced and unqualified buyers, because they have given a low opinion of value. Finally, this list, when sequenced in price order, will be your priority list of whom to call back first for a second showing. We leave the lowest opinions of value for last.

As a final note, solicit opinions from real estate brokers as well. These opinions, assuming these brokers are active in your defined geography, should be given great weight in determining market value. Here's a hint that could really give you an insight of how knowledgeable these brokers are. If you get opinions of value well outside the range of your excellent market research and the opinions of other buyers, you can conclude that such brokers are not well-educated in your defined geography. If you haven't hired a broker yet, don't hire these unenlightened souls. Some agents will intentionally exaggerate or puff the value estimate in order to lull a seller into signing up with them.

Sell the Appointment

Be prepared for people who call on your mailers or your signs. Don't talk too much; your goal is to get the appointment. You can't sell a house over the phone; you can only sell an appointment. Clearly, you're motivated to sell the property, because you've advertised the sale. No matter how desperate you are to sell, resist the temptation to sell the house too much over the phone. As a matter of fact, if you're a blabbermouth, have someone else take the calls.

A third party with less emotional involvement can be more effective. The only thing you want to sell over the phone is an appointment to show up at the open house. Only if the buyer insists that he can't make the open house do you arrange a private showing. Again, the conversation should be as brief as possible, giving the minimum amount of information, repeatedly asking the potential buyer when she would like to see the house and using what we call the "alternative-choice" close; for example, "Would you like to see the house now, or would later today be better?" If the buyer answers with a question about the house, you reply briefly and press again with another alternate-choice question ("Would 6 P.M. work, or would 8 P.M. be better?"). Keep pressing for the appointment, and say as little as possible. Remember, it's almost impossible to sell a house over the phone, so don't try!

Grand Opening: Big Splash or Testing the Water?

The whole idea here is to get as many buyers and even the nosey neighbors into the house at the same time. For those parents who have two children close in age, we're sure you can appreciate how a little competition goes a long way. Even if your best buyer is in the house with a neighbor who may just be sizing you up to figure out what his house is worth, your good buyers don't know this. The extra looker will eventually help flush out what the real buyers' highest price is in a shorter amount of time, since they may believe they're not the only people interested.

We have had numerous clients that have wanted to top dollar, yet were afraid to let everyone know. It may not be intuitive, but this approach is counterproductive. Making the biggest possible splash into the pool of available properties will bring in the most action at the *same* time and ultimately procure the highest possible price with the least amount of headaches. Ironically, when done properly, this will occur in the least amount of time as well. It's sort of like finding the right fishing spot, lowering your hooks and getting the hungriest and most aggressive (and often the largest) fish to bite right from the beginning.

Market interest tends to decline exponentially as weekends tick by. The reason for this is that the excitement of a new listing wanes. Experienced buyers shopping the market have all lost a house right after it was listed because they hesitated. If this hasn't happened to your buyer yet, it probably means that your buyer hasn't seen enough houses yet.

Lastly, buyers tend to get skeptical about why a house hasn't sold if it's been on the market for months as opposed to weeks. Always answer this question in terms of open houses; for example, "Mr. and Mrs. Seller, how long has the house been for sale?"

We would respond in two ways. Firstly, we always consider a property's number of open houses done at a particular price as the time on the market. If your property has been for sale for six months and you recently adjusted the price and this weekend is the first open house at this price, you should say "This is the first weekend we're holding an open house at this price." If you haven't had any price changes, then say "This is only our second open house," even if the property has been for sale for months, provided that of course this is true.

The Open House: It's Show Time!

Hey, That Guy Is in My Fishing Slick

On the day of the actual open house you may notice that one of your competitors is also having an open house. Why not take advantage of this and piggyback on their action? Unless the homes are exactly alike, they probably won't mind. The activity that the competitor has put into his open house is free exposure to you if you know how to take advantage of this tactfully.

Fishing tactics have taught us a few things about getting the other guys' leads. We recall being on an ocean fishing trip where the captain would strategically look for other boats (as we would troll for open houses) in the area where we planned to fish. He would make sure to gauge the direction of the current (flow of traffic through the home). It would always be to our advantage to be in his fishing slick. This is where a fishing boat has anchored up and has started to put bait into the water to attract the fish. These fishing slicks can extend for miles. Our captain would be cautious enough to be at a distance greater than a shotgun blast, yet close enough for the fish to get into our fishing slick. Oh, the time saved, and not to mention the extra exposure to our hooks! Using the same strategy, it would be wise to have an extra person driving around to check out your real estate fishing slick and make sure to maximize your directional sign exposure.

Second, we highly recommend making sure your competitors aren't getting in your slick. Specifically, at the major intersections, make sure no one has kicked down your sign or is blocking the view. Play fair, and don't block the competitor's signs either. However, it's perfectly okay to preempt their strategy by placing signs at a high-visibility intersection or two. This game plan really needs to be addressed a day or two before your first open house. Studies have shown that the primary way buyers find the home they ultimately purchase is simply having been in the neighborhood and driven by the sign. Every broker knows this tightly keep secret.

We've statistically measured the ultimate cause-and-effect relationships between advertising and the simple effective use of signs. Check with your local municipalities and be prepared to pay the advertising fee (fine) they may charge you. Most building inspectors don't work on weekends (hint, hint). However, some municipalities can impose a rather steep fee for noncompliance. Consider the cost, and be prepared to pay for fine as a cost of doing business. If the fine is too high, check out what the big-player local brokers are doing to circumvent the problem. For example, some villages allow signs on a car but not on the sidewalks. Do your due diligence, and use common sense so that you don't violate any traffic ordinances. Again, checking out the competition a weekend or two before you launch onto the market is one of the greatest time investments you can make toward the success of your sale.

The Longer the Better When Facing Off Against Your Competition. Make sure your open house goes for at least one hour longer than your competition. Most buyers with an average IQ tend to forget the house after they have seen more than five others. So, being the last on the list is the position to aim for.

We recall buyers that couldn't remember the color of the kitchen cabinets of the house they saw in the morning and even less about the house they saw last weekend. Knowing that buyers are looking at hundreds of details per house makes this not a matter of genius but of how much information they can process and recall. This is why your flier is so important. Furthermore, simply asking the buyer how many homes they've seen over the weekend will acquaint you with their confusion level. We've found that buyers who have looked at more than five properties per day tend to blur the details of the various homes. A prudent seller can help keep things clear in the buyer's mind by making things as simple as possible.

For example, most amateur sellers tend to overtalk and oversell. The buyers' heads are so full of information that it is effective to keep it clear from the beginning what they're looking at. Rounding out information and making it easy to remember is what the process here is all about. If your house has a 3,125-square-foot floor plan, simply say it's a bit over 3,000 square feet. If your MLS listing is priced at $297,000, simply say that the price is just under $300,000. This applies to all the questions the buyer asks you. Don't volunteer information during the show time at the open house or at a private showing. Studies have shown that rarely does a buyer buy a house without a second viewing. Wait until the buyers have a taste of what your property offers them; at that point the details can emerge. A confused mind does not buy!

Have a Polaroid Handy

Have an old-style Polaroid camera available for buyers to take their own photos and notes. You should take a picture of the potential buyer in front of the house and give them the photo to remember it by. Also, take a photo of the buyer, and keep a picture for yourself to remember the people you are later negotiating with over the phone. These strategies should be used only if and when you feel that the opportunity is present. We would recommend you do this at a time when you identify this particular buyer as a good candidate.

We recall a broker in our area who would claim to give his open house attendees a quart of ice cream in the summer so they would have to head home after his open house and not be able to keep shopping. A quart of ice cream would not necessarily prohibit all buyers from doing their due diligence. However, the point is that doing open houses after the other guys have closed up is definitely an exposure advantage to keep in mind. Serious buyers often tire out and simply want to end the ordeal of dizzying tours with the finalization of successfully finding their best choice. If you're the last home they see that meets their needs, you might just get the "Okay, I'm done shopping, this one meets the criteria, let's make a deal" buyer. Men fall into this category two to one over women.

The Logical Showing

The best logical order of the showing of a house is actually not logical at all. Most sellers and agents walk people right from the front door to each room, confidently announcing, "This is the kitchen," as if buyers don't recognize a kitchen when they see one. The tendency is to talk too much and get in the way of the show.

In fact, there's a much more effective way to do this, as you will discover shortly.

A Walk in the Park Holding Hands

Starting with the end in mind, a house showing should end up at the kitchen table where friends gather. So, starting with the outside first avoids the habitual mistake of leaving it for last. The problem with this is the uncomfortable and awkward feeling of what to do next when you find yourself outside at the end of a showing. The temptation to show certain features of your house in the order that you like can conflict with the more effective strategy that we'll lay out for you. It sounds counterintuitive, but showing the outside first and the best interior features should take priority.

Some men feel that they want to show off the systems of the house. This is a major bore for the wife, who usually is the greater decision maker. Save the systems for the middle of the showing. For example, when showing the outside of the house, consider the better view.

Counterclockwise or clockwise may give a different view and have a more appealing flow. As objectively as possible, try walking the outside of the property with someone else first and slowly make an assessment of which direction will be the directional flow of choice. Then stick to it. If your house has a golf-course view that's most enhanced by an approach from a clockwise direction, use that as part of your tour. Keep in mind that this is not a follow-the-leader game. As tempting as it is to show off and lead the way, studies have shown that buyers will be influenced most strongly when they discover the beauties of the view for themselves, with you out of the picture. At these highlights it's effective to pause and let silence be your best friend. Buyers need to take in the view for a moment. One of our favorite lines at this highlight point about the beauty is to simply ask them, "Do you hear that?" They will ask, "Hear what?" You say, "Exactly . . .

nothing, just peace and quiet." A little humor at the right time can also make this a memorable experience.

After the outside showing, take your prospects through the front door. Some sellers make the mistake of taking buyers through the same door that they're used to using.

For example, going through the garage into the laundry room into the living room is fine for friends and family; however, the best first impression should be exactly that. If your house has an impressive deck with a magnificent view, then making that the first stop on the tour will pay off. Pausing along the way at the sweet spots is always a big plus. Keep in mind that it's best to cover the best areas first and to show perhaps the less interesting ones second and to end off at the kitchen table.

Sellers make their biggest mistakes when they pace the tour. Let the buyers start to move away from this space as a hint to you as to when it is time to move on. Again, to go slow is to go fast. If you have a spacious home and more than one group of buyers shows up, consider having zone assistants. Have each floor or area handled by one person. The person handling the last part of the showing should always ask the buyers if they would like to see the home again. We have strategized that the last person should also be the one who is best at dealing with people. This person then would handle the entire re-show and the later negotiations.

Lastly, if your house is a colonial or two-story with a basement and your buyers are somewhat elderly, don't show the basement before the second floor. It has happened that a mature buyer has had a stroke because after viewing the first floor and then the basement, his two-story climb to the second floor was more than he could handle.

Psychology of Selling

In order to sell your house, you have to understand what makes people tick. Everyone is different, so you have to ask a lot of questions and be patient to get a feel for what will motivate your buyer. Most sellers assume that it's either price or falling in love with the house. While the bargain and love of a house are certainly factors, there are many more things that motivate people. Here are five:

1. **Fear.** If your buyer speaks out of fear-based thinking or risk aversion, use that as a motivator. Discuss with him the safety

of the investment, how low the crime is in the neighborhood or how well the house is built. Find out what his concerns are and answer all of his questions. Offer a homebuyer's warranty to cover anything that might break. If he's afraid of making a mistake, offer a 72-hour right to cancel the contract. The more you can alleviate his fear, the more likely he'll be willing to commit to buying.

2. **Love.** If your buyer is a romantic, sell him on the dream of buying your home. Play to his emotions rather than his intellect. If it's his first home, recount the memories you've had in the home with your family. Try to get him to imagine a Thanksgiving Day feast in the dining room. Paint a picture of his daughter walking down the staircase in her prom dress. Talk about how he and his wife will grow old together in rocking chairs on the front porch.

3. **Greed.** If buyers are motivated by greed, they'll be enticed by a good deal, especially if they think they have negotiated the deal. Appeal to the fact that you've spent a lot of money on repairs and improvements that will inure to their benefit. If you are pricing it cheap because you haven't made improvements, discuss with them what a tremendous bargain they will be getting on the price.

4. **Ego and Vanity.** The multibillion dollar infomercial product business is built on looking beautiful and thin. If someone pulls up in a nice car and is dressed well, appeal to the vanity factor. If the neighborhood has prestige, remind buyers of that fact. If you are near a particular country club or shopping mall, remind them of what may appeal to them. Believe it or not, some people like to brag about what they paid for things. If you have expensive or unique appliances, imported hardwood floors and the like, give them some ammunition they can brag to their friends about. Make sure the property information flyer lists all of these features so that they can show off to their friends.

5. **Intelligence.** Some people like to fancy themselves as smart and sensible. If you find one of these types, appeal to their intellect. Remind them of features and benefits of the property and what a value it is for the money. If they're looking at more expensive properties, remind them of how smart it is to live

within their budget and save money. Convince them a more expensive house is excessive.

Start by building rapport with sellers. People are more likely to buy from someone they trust and like than from someone they don't. While they certainly won't buy just because you hit it off, they are more likely to go to your competition if you completely rub them the wrong way. Avoid controversial topics like religion and politics. And most importantly, try to listen more than you talk. The sure sign of a bad salesman is one who talks his customers to death rather than asking questions to find out what they care about. If you get lost on what to say, recall the six fundamental questions—who, what, where, when, why and how.

Please, Make Yourself at Home!

The first 30 seconds is a critical time at any point of sale. Make sure to have your best smile on with a plan to lead buyers to the outside showing of the property. Remember to be a guide and point out the direction for them to take, but don't lead the way. A few simple comments on the outside features can break the ice. Follow their lead and keep your comments about the property simple and clear. The less you say the better. If they are talkative, then naturally follow suit if it feels right to you. As you circle back to the front of the house, open the door and let them go in first and say "Please, make yourselves at home." What a nice way to start off the interior part of the show.

Aside from the order of which floors to show first, as we discussed, let them lead the way for the most part. It's almost like an Easter-egg hunt. The parents let the kids find and discover for themselves, yet the parents will point out the features as they get near them. It not only is more interesting for the buyers and exciting for them to discover features of the home, it is also more memorable as well. Buyers often have an agenda of priorities.

Seeing who is the leader of the buyers' group will tell you one of the most valuable bits of information about the leader and usually identify the decision maker. Giving this person the most respect and attention is most efficient, since she will probably have the most say in the purchase. Watch the interaction between the husband and wife or others in the buyers' group. This will often tell much more than the words do. The showing of affection is a good sign, especially if they are obvious about it. If the buyers go off in different directions, simply ask them if we can all stay together. It's important to let them lead the way, but you must stay in control of the direction of the flow. Some sellers know their home better than anyone and feel that a particular flow would be best. That's fine as long as it ends up with an offer of some sort of snack or refreshment at the kitchen table. This allows them to envision themselves in the home for a minute to try it on for size.

The kitchen is the heart of the home for most people and where decisions involving the family and finances are often made. So ending up in the kitchen to discuss your house is the perfect place to start informal negotiations. Offering them a seat as you begin to sit is a great test. If they easily sit down with you, you can be sure that they are either interested in your house or just tired of looking. This part of the show is relaxing for the buyers. Don't discuss price negotiations yet. Always discuss the price negotiations at the end. We'll cover this in the next chapter. As for now, it's time to get to know the buyer.

The Placebo Effect

An interesting tactic to get a buzz going at your open house is to serve virgin tropical drinks, but don't tell anyone there's no alcohol in them. People will psychologically (and sometimes physically) feel good about their experience at your open house and remember it like a good party.

Are They Qualified?

Two things you want to make sure of are whether the person is qualified financially and logically to buy your house. *Financially* means whether they have the means to buy and can qualify for a loan. *Logically* means whether they are in the mode of being ready emotionally to buy a house. Have they seen enough houses and discussed it enough among themselves to be ready to make a decision? We will deal with both in this section.

Will the Real Buyers Please Step Forward

When prospective buyers come through the house we need to qualify them by asking the right questions. Remember, we're looking for buyers who are ready, able and willing. The acronym TYNHOW is the correct order of questions to ask your potential buyers to screen them out. It can be easily remembered by thinking of the Tin Man character from the Wizard of Oz.

T—What (T)?

Y—Why (Y)?

N—When (N)?

H—How (H)?

O—Who (O)?

W—Where (W)?

Asking the prospective buyers these qualifying questions should take place after you've offered them a re-show of the property (as discussed below). It's pointless to qualify buyers who aren't interested in your home. The litmus test for genuine interest is simply offering them a second showing of the house. This isn't necessary if the prospective buyers are obviously interested. If the prospective buyers look at your house in less than 10 minutes and start heading for their car, then simply saying, "Thank you," and handing them an extra flier to pass out to their friends will suffice. Studies have shown that prospective buyers who take longer than 25 minutes to view a 2,000-square-foot house are probably very interested. At this point, the re-show offering should be presented, as you now start to take the lead and point out the finer details of the home. It is at the end of the re-show that the qualifying questions should be asked. As informally and as friendly as possible, ask the following questions.

What Are You Looking For?   If the prospective buyers hesitate, making a joke about how this home is just the right one for them would be appropriate. Asking them what kind of home they have now and how this one compares is often a great icebreaker. You'll be amazed at the amount of information that the prospective buyers will give you. Naturally, you will want to reiterate the noteworthy features your house offers over theirs in your closing presentation when attempting to get the prospective buyers up to the highest possible price. Remember, it's emotions that will motivate the prospective buyers, but it's the logic that will get them to commit.

Custom-tailoring your sales pitch is highly effective and necessary to remind the buyers why this home is the best one for them.

Why Are You Moving?   This question often reveals less obvious motivating factors behind the prospective buyers' decision to move. Studies have shown that the wives tend to have a clearer and greater understanding as to why they are undertaking this move. Moving has been notoriously one of the most stressful events in a family's journey through life. Easing their anxieties through the reiteration of their motivation to move at the appropriate time is priceless. It's perfectly okay to take notes on your prospective buyers' information sheet as they tell you their story. The reason for their move will often reveal the deadline by which they have to move. Asking them is not offensive, because most buyers will appreciate the fact that you care enough to ask.

When Are You Looking to Move?   This piece of information is probably the most relevant you need to know about your prospective buyer. You want to know their timeline, so you need to know whether they are under the gun or taking their sweet time.

Ask the presumptive question about when they'd like to move in, such as "Mr. Buyer, is moving before or after the upcoming holiday better for you?" Most buyers who have sold a property know exactly the time frame they are working within. Being able to accommodate it can make a big difference between your house and the other options they have. For example, if your house is vacant and they're looking at other homes in which sellers need to find a place to move, then this advantage should be exploited. However, you need to know their time frame to exploit it. We're not encouraging you to use their timeline against them, but letting them know how your occupancy date can meet their needs is often one of the first things that should be discussed, prior to the price.

How Long Have They Been Looking?   Buyers are like tomatoes. If they're too green they're not ready; if they have been around too long, they get rotten! Studies have shown that it's a matter of two factors that will determine if buyers are seasoned and ready to purchase: first, the length of time they have actually been looking. Most buyers need between 3 and 12 weekends to feel confident enough that they've properly shopped the market. Let's remember that there are only so many houses a buyer can effectively look at and remember over a given weekend. If the prospective buyer has looked for less than 3 or more than 12 weekends he is either unripe or rotten.

If your buyer is unripe, he hasn't looked at enough houses to buy yet, and a follow up phone call in a few weeks would be highly prudent. For example, we've had buyers that looked at the home that they ultimately purchased during their first weekend of shopping. However, they continued to look at other houses for months to exhaust their options before making a purchasing decision. Inviting them back for the re-show, just to give the house a second chance, has proven successful many times in the case of the unripe buyer. On the other hand, prospective buyers that have been looking for too long may have a latent problem. For example, they may have champagne taste and a beer budget, or, more commonly have relatives or friends that have homes they wished they could afford, but can't.

The second factor is the frequency in which the prospective buyer shops for homes. The best buyers look every weekend. Their motivation is so strong that they'll even look at homes during their lunch breaks from work. These buyers should be given preference and your fullest attention. Prospective buyers that look every other

Sometimes a Second Look Is All They Need

Patti was a very enthusiastic and motivated buyer, and was the decision maker in her family when it came to finding a home. Patti came to us the first week she started looking. The first property she saw was absolutely the best for her, but she wasn't ready to make a decision yet because she had no point of reference. After five months of shopping for homes, she came back to us, frustrated that none of the homes were just right for her. Coincidentally, the first home she looked at had been under contract and fell through. We suggested that she go back and look at the home again. She was very reluctant, since she had already crossed that home off her list. Since she trusted us, she agreed to have a second look at the home and ultimately purchase it. This time, she saw the home through the eyes of an experienced and well-ripened buyer. It was truly amazing at how different the home appeared this time around. It wasn't that Patti had lowered her standards, it was just that after shopping the market she was able to appreciate the value that this home offered. Like everything in life, it is a matter of relative appreciation that only comes through experience and good timing.

weekend tend to be moderately serious buyers. People who look once a month are just not motivated enough to spend your time and energy on; they're in the tire-kicker category. Plan a follow-up phone call to these people about every two weeks to see if their frequency of shopping has stepped up. A final point here worth mentioning is that the more frequently a buyer looks at houses, the more likely it is he will be your best candidate.

Who Are Your Decision Makers? You want to make sure you're talking to the right people who are involved in making the decision to purchase. When showing the house, usually the most important person to talk to is one of the people to whom you're showing the home. Hopefully the group is manageable. In the case of a husband and wife, watch to see who takes the lead. The leader is usually the one who asks the most questions or raises the most objections. While objections may seem negative, they represent a person who has interest. The person who is quiet and doesn't ask any questions is generally not as interested as someone who raises a lot of issues. The point we're making is that your focus needs to be primarily on the person who's the decision maker, who takes the lead herself. So watch who leads the group. As obvious as this may seem, you may miss it with so many things going on at an open house. Focusing on this person will tend to yield the greatest results and save the most time when the negotiating process starts, which in our opinion is the moment the buyers agree to a second look.

Respect the Mavens

Very often buyers will have a so-called expert they are relying on for information and guidance about the purchase of their home. We call these people the mavens, and they are generally a friend who is a real estate broker or a relative who knows a little about real estate (but not as much as they think they know). Since this person will have an influence on the decision-making process, be sure to treat this person with respect. The last thing you want to do is alienate someone your buyer relies on for advice.

Where Are You Coming From? You'll want to know where the prospective buyers are moving from. Buyers that live on busy streets are used to them and may have no problem if your house is on a busy street. Depending on where the buyer is coming from, certain features of the house may be more or less attractive to them. For example, if they're coming from an area that is near transportation and shopping, the fact that your house shares those same features would be a plus to emphasize. So, keep in mind things that are common denominators that you can use to your advantage. Don't assume that a spacious back yard is necessarily a plus for a buyer. It may represent too much work.

The flip side of the equation is that you should not assume that because buyers have certain features in their current home they are satisfied with them. For example, if they have a two-story home, they may be looking for a ranch because they're thinking about their golden years. Don't make assumptions; ask questions. The best question to ask is, "What do you like or dislike about where you currently live?" This open-ended question allows them to discuss not just their specific home, but it allows for elaboration about their current local geography and amenities. One final point worth mentioning is that you shouldn't overemphasize the amenities in your neighborhood until you've asked your buyers their opinion about the amenities you're speaking about. For example, in a highly rated school district, seniors with no children may think they're overpaying in taxes to subsidize the education of other people's children.

Buy or Die

Most people take a laid-back approach to selling their house, allowing people to look, and then walk right out the door, with a friendly, "Ya'll come back, now, you hear." Most sales experts will tell you that it takes seven or more contacts with a prospective buyer to get him to sign on the dotted line. Thus, your job is to get your prospective buyers in a conversation and/or viewing of the house as many times as you can. The more times they come to view the house and the longer they stay, the greater chance you have of making a deal.

Once you've developed a list of potential buyers from your open house and calls from your marketing efforts, keep following up until your prospects buy or die, so to speak. Most of the sellers will not be calling their buyers because they have not read this book and don't know the most powerful tool in the toolbox—the recall for the re-show. Call up each and every potential lead on the Monday after the open house and ask them if they would like to schedule a "re-showing" of the house. Undoubtedly they'll have looked at many homes over the weekend and will have likely forgotten what your house looks like. When you call, try using a memory trigger with the buyers to help them remember the house. Don't just reference "the four-bedroom house on Elm Street," but rather "the blue colonial-style house with the _____ (insert most unique and memorable feature).

Remember, the only thing you sell on the phone is an appointment to view or re-view the property. If the buyers decline your invitation for a re-showing, the best thing to ask them at this point is what they liked and disliked most about your house and what price they think the house will realistically sell for. Feedback is the breakfast of champions. It is this aggregate feedback that we are searching for. You'll also start to get a feel for how ripe or unripe your buyer is based on his comments and opinions of price. If they are way off the mark on range of values (either too high or low), then you can probably stop wasting time with this person and move on to someone else, unless of course, the buyer is too ripe. Put prospects on your call back list for every other Thursday night until the either buy . . . or die!

Chapter Summary

- It's all about driving people to the open house. The more people who show up, the more competition and interest you will create for your house.

- Take it slowly, and have a plan for showing the house to prospective buyers.

- Ask the right questions to qualify your prospective buyers.

- Follow up on prospective buyers and offer them a re-showing of the property.

CHAPTER 9

Negotiating the Deal—
You've Got a Buyer,
So Don't Blow It!

Let us never negotiate out of fear, but let us never fear to negotiate.
   —John F. Kennedy, "Inaugural Address" (January 20, 1961)

This chapter is perhaps the most important one because it's where most sellers and their agents fall down when it comes to getting the deal closed. Remember, it's not just about spurring interest in your house; it's about getting the right offers so that you can sign the contract and close. This chapter will discuss negotiating, how to deal with buyers, and how to avoid those mistakes that cause deals to fall apart.

Let's define the term. *To negotiate* means "to confer with another or others in order to come to terms or reach an agreement." Beyond this simple definition, negotiation is a technique in business transactions that people use to try to get what they want or need from a particular business dealing. To some, negotiating comes as naturally as breathing or eating. To others, it's a skill learned and perfected through years of practice and experience. The great thing is that anyone can learn to negotiate. You might even be doing it in your everyday life without even realizing it.

Do You Have What It Takes To Be a Skilled Negotiator?

Of course you do; everyone does. You're at an advantage now because you're learning the tools that you'll use to perfect this skill. Think about it. You obviously have a desire to succeed, because you're reading this book. You want to be a better negotiator. You're willing to practice and learn the techniques that powerful negotiators use to get what they want. That's the first step.

You also understand the importance of negotiating. You aren't willing to settle for whatever the real estate world sends your way. Read on to learn the three keys to successful negotiation. Learning and practicing these skills are an investment in you as a real estate entrepreneur. You'll increase your net worth by honing in on your ability to get better prices, secure more clients and close more favorable deals.

The Three Keys to Successful Negotiation

Build Rapport

This is the foundation on which you will build any given negotiation. You must establish yourself as a trustworthy, likeable person. Why else would people be willing to work with you?

You are at your best, most influential self when people trust you. People want to hear what you have to say. They respect your opinion. They believe you.

Some people skip this step. They don't think they need to build rapport. They jump right into the negotiation. Do you know what other people usually think? They find those people annoying. They seem as though they're just trying to beat the other person down. They're insincere, and everyone knows it.

On the other hand, those who master rapport building aren't seen this way at all. Instead of thinking that you're trying to beat someone over the head with your price demands, they see that you're trying to work with them. They want the deal to work, because they like and trust you.

Determine What They Want

It sounds simple enough. But it can be a difficult skill to master. You have to get good at finding out what people want; how else will you negotiate with them? Once you know what they want, you have a tool to bargain with. You know their end goal. Now, you just have to get them to see how their goal and your goal can work towards the same end.

Some people think that salesmanship is a sleazy, smarmy practice. On the contrary, we don't think manipulation or lying is what negotiating is all about. But we do want to teach you to recognize your bargaining chips and know how to use them.

It's human nature that people just don't want to give up on what they want. There's an old expression, "Buyers are liars, and sellers are storytellers." Does this mean that people are inherently bad or have malicious intentions? Of course not, but people won't always volunteer the truth about what they really want.

Once you know what they want, you can create a win-win situation. You will sell your house for a fair price, and the buyers will get a good value for their money. You want to make money while solving their problem. Their problem is that they need to buy a house. No lying, no manipulating, and no sleaziness involved. It's just negotiating!

Find a Resolution

This can also be difficult, but it's the most important step. What good is it to negotiate a great deal, only to have the buyer back out on you? You need to find a resolution that's going to work for both of you.

In order to do this, you need to learn and develop the communication techniques that we'll discuss in the next section. You must be able to listen to the sellers, understand what type of people they are, and use an approach that will work best with their personalities.

A resolution can't be one-sided or unfair; it should honestly work for both parties. Both should come away feeling that a problem has been solved. As we delve deeper into mastering negotiating, you'll see how communications skills and psychology play an important role in helping to find resolutions and convey them in a way that's logical and convincing to the person on the other side of the negotiating table.

Building Rapport

Establishing commonality is an important factor in rapport building. To establish commonality is much the same as it sounds; you want to show people you have something in common with them.

How is this helpful in a negotiation? It helps to establish trust. Naturally, we feel more comfortable with someone we can relate to. Feeling we have something in common with people automatically creates a sense that we can relate to them.

People Like People Who Are Like Them

People generally like to deal with people they like; and people generally like people who are like them. Try starting the prenegotiating by finding common ground between you and the buyers. Common likes and dislikes, background, and communication styles will help bridge the gap between stranger and friend. Ask questions to elicit the proper responses, so you can try to move the conversation in a direction of friendly bonding.

Match and mirror the communication style of the other parties. For example, if they talk slow and you talk fast, slow it down for them. If they like to gesture with their hands a lot, match these gestures. If they talk loudly, you should talk loudly. If they talk softly, you should talk softly. Don't worry, they won't think you're poking fun; most people aren't even aware of the way they're communicating. They will see commonality, and they will feel that something about you looks very familiar to them.

Don't Blow It

While you're trying to establish a commonality and trust with people, you don't want to blow the whole deal by offending them.

This one can be difficult because many of the things we talk about when we're nervous are so ingrained. We may not even realize that what feels natural to us could be offensive to someone else. When you've established that trust, don't fall into the trap of getting comfortable and blurting out something that could put the other person on edge. They're not your friends; you can't talk openly about certain things just because you've connected.

Avoid these topics in your business dealings and negotiations:

- Politics
- Religion
- Race
- War

- Sex
- Controversial Current Events

This list certainly isn't exhaustive. But it's important to avoid these topics. Even if you think the person you're speaking to is a Republican, don't make a crack about Democrats. How do you know his dear Auntie Mae isn't a Democrat? Don't make a comment about how glad you are that you saw on the news last night that a certain criminal was sent to death row. Maybe you're talking to someone who doesn't believe in the death penalty.

You just never know. Take the safe route to avoid throwing up any road blocks that would make the person think, "I really don't agree on that." That creates an objection; the exact opposite of your goal.

Where and When to Negotiate

When to Negotiate

After the open house is done and you have re-shown the property or have a prospective buyer willing to start negotiating price and terms, you need to think about the best time to start the negotiating process. Like an after-dinner mint, there's an appropriate time to start the process. Studies have shown that negotiating while people are at work is probably the worst time to have the discussion. The reason for this is they are distracted with other responsibilities and aren't focused on the task at hand. Assuming that you're going to negotiating with the decision maker, the ideal time would be after dinner and, if they have children, after the children have gone to bed. The reasons for this are obvious; you want their full and undivided attention.

If they sound tired, ask them if it's a good time to discuss price and terms. You need to respect their schedule and their ability to allow enough time to fully discuss elements that will be pertinent to a successful transaction. This also applies to you yourself; pick an appropriate time where you're fresh and can give your full attention to the negotiating process. It's crucial for you to pay close attention to the details of the conversation. The slightest and most innocent comments can often lead to discovering important issues that need to be considered. For example, the buyers' ability to purchase may be contingent upon the sale of their present home. This is often referred to as the "domino effect." Your buyer's ability to purchase is often a function of their buyer's ability to purchase the house your buyer is selling. If that buyer is also selling a property, the chain of transactions are ultimately only as strong as the weakest link in the chain. So, listening carefully to all of the details that your buyers are willing to provide must be done in a quiet environment where you can focus on the contingencies within the offer itself.

Where to Negotiate

There are two schools of thought on setting. The first is for the experienced professional. Negotiations should take place face to face for those professionals who are comfortable enough in the three key areas of that realm. First, your ability to recall the due-diligence information will be paramount. Secondly, your ability to remain calm and objective is a function of how nervous you may or may not get, considering the magnitude of the amount of money involved. Some people have a difficult time keeping things in perspective and they need to think in terms of percentages instead of dollar amounts of large-ticket items. Third and last, your ability to control and observe body language is the primary reason for negotiating face to face.

Here are a few simple tips on face-to-face body language negotiations. It has been said that the majority of communications between two parties are more often a matter of nonverbal clues and signals. Studies have shown that you must monitor your own body language, so that you don't give the wrong impression. For example, if an issue is one that may be uncomfortable for you, then it is crucial to maintain direct eye contact and avoid touching your face (especially your mouth and nose) at the moment after you respond to the sensitive question. Honesty is the best policy, because the truth usually bubbles to the surface before you get to the closing table. Keeping this in mind, it's imperative that you directly and honestly answer any questions in the simplest and shortest way possible. This isn't the time to tell stories that will probably be used against you at a later time. The biggest mistake even professionals make is the tendency to talk too much and not listen enough. Remember the old adage, "God gave us two ears and one mouth for a reason." We should listen twice as much as we talk. This last statement is probably the most important part of negotiating, since it will yield the greatest amount of information that you can use to your advantage to achieve the highest possible price.

Be Careful Where You Sit

If you don't want to intimidate your buyers, don't sit in the driver's seat, that is, the head of the table. If you were selling a car, you would let the buyer drive so that he thinks he's in control of the situation. If you take the passenger seat and let the buyer talk, you'll get more information out of him. Try to observe whether the husband or the wife sits at the head of the table. This will give you a clue about who's making the ultimate decision. However, studies have also shown that the mother of the house usually has the most influence over the decision-making process in the family home.

The second school of thought on where to negotiate is for the nonprofessional who may be too nervous to negotiate face to face. In this case, the phone is a better way to communicate. We have found that two heads are better than one. That does not mean that two people should be on the phone at the same time with a prospective buyer. One person should handle the conversation exclusively. We have found it helpful for a second person, someone you trust, perhaps your partner, to be listening in on the conversation. You would be amazed at how many times two people listening to the same conversation will hear two different things as well as things the other person missed. The reason for this is that many people engaged in negotiations will be thinking of what they will say next. It's human nature not to listen, but rather to think about what you'll say next. We've found that after thousands of successful transactions, it's imperative to take copious notes on as many details of the conversation as possible. This will force you to listen twice as much as you talk. Furthermore, your closing part of the negotiating must emphasize the selling features of your home that most accommodate your buyer's needs, desires, and dreams.

If your negotiations are taking place face to face, it's perfectly fine to take as many notes as you feel are important. This, however, should be done with tact and common sense. You don't want your buyers to feel that they are under oath in a deposition. The goal is to make the buyers feel as though you truly care . . . and you should! You're looking for the win-win scenario; the highest and best user of your property is the one you can confidently count on to pay the highest possible price. It is also the one you don't want to lose, because losing this buyer will typically result in a selling price that will be significantly lower with the next buyer in line.

Allow for the human element of the honest, misspoken mistakes of verbiage. Many well-intentioned parties mistake what they mean to say and do not even notice. So, measure twice and cut once, and be crystal clear on the key issues.

The Power of Probing Questions

Along the lines of our discussion about listening more than talking, questions are the key to making this process easier. If you ask a lot of questions, you're forced to listen and you make the buyer feel important. By using the TYNHOW questions from Chapter 8—and any other questions you can think of—you remain in control of the negotiations. Whenever you get lost, ask an open-ended question of your prospective buyer and listen actively to the answer; for example, "Tell me about some of the other properties you've looked at." This question can be followed up with "What were the features you liked best and worst about these other houses?" Or try "How does this compare with the other houses?" Open-ended questions like these get the buyer talking so that you can find out more about what they're looking for. The answers to these questions will not only tell you how the buyer likes your house, but how ripe or unripe your buyer is at this time. A buyer can go from unripe (not quite ready to buy just yet) to a ripe buyer in a matter of weeks, especially if he has dedicated a large chunk of time to shop the market.

The Test Close

The test close is a powerful technique for moving buyers along the path from interest to contract. A test close is a question that presumes a purchasing decision of the buyer and/or gets them moving in the direction of the yes momentum. Asking questions that elicit an obvious "yes" or other positive response will help lead your prospective buyer in the direction of a positive purchasing decision. For example, asking leading questions such as "The schools are great in this district, aren't they?" get the buyer nodding his head up and down in a positive manner. The more questions you can ask that solicit a positive response, the more you'll move the buyer toward a close.

In addition, presumptive questions are also powerful to subconsciously implant the idea of a sale in the buyer's mind. For example, a question such as, "Where would you place the television in the living room?" presumes the buyer has already made the decision to purchase. Multiple choice questions are also effective, such as "When would you like to move in, before or after the holidays?" These timelines get the buyer thinking in terms of definiteness of a decision in favor of buying your house.

The Three-Letter Word that Can Make You Thousands

The take-away point here is reminding yourself to uncover how you want the negotiations to end. It always works well when both sides feel as if they have achieved a fair ending point to the negotiations. Specifically, we like to call this the midway point just as if John Wayne were negotiating with another cowboy.

The John Wayne method is often used whether you are negotiating face to face, on the phone, or by faxing offers and counteroffers back and forth between real estate brokers. The method is simple— ready, aim, fire. One party offers X, the other offers Y, then you split the difference. This is the common meet in the middle method of wrapping up a negotiation.

The key here is to get the buyers to start with their highest possible offer. Obviously, the higher the offer within your bracketed range of values that you have already determined from your comps book, the better. If your buyer starts beneath the range of bracketed values then simply decline to provide a counteroffer and politely request that the offer be resubmitted. If you're face to face or on the phone, then say, "I'm sorry, but you'll have to do better than that."

Just like the preparation that goes into baking a cake, the key to success when negotiating a big-ticket item is the preparation that takes place before the monetary figures are discussed. Price should be the last thing that gets negotiated in a transaction. This will give you the time to develop the rapport and trust that become the foundation upon which your relationship with the buyer will be built. So, it is here at the starting point of price negotiations where you can use one of the most critical and yet cost-free strategies that will help you achieve the highest possible price.

Focusing on the buyer's starting offer should be prefaced by assisting the buyer to get into the right state of mind. Assuming the buyer will make an offer, it's imperative that you use the magical three-letter word before he gives you a first offer. This word is "yet." The way this should be used is very simple. As soon as the buyer hints at getting a feel of how flexible you may or may not be on price, your response should always be the same, regardless of whether it directly answers his question. For example, the buyer asks, "Mr. Jones, how flexible are you on price?" or "Are you negotiable on price?" Your response should be, "We haven't accepted any offers yet; however, we do plan on selling the property in the near future." Whether you have an offer or not is irrelevant. It's true and has the added benefit of giving the buyer the impression that you're entertaining more than one offer. The truth is that any time a buyer inquires about your house, you have an interested party. It's only when an offer is actually accepted in writing that you have a meeting of the minds. Until then, all interested parties are possible candidates for purchase. The power of the word "yet" can't be understated.

As simple as this may seem, at the time of negotiations most sellers lose their nerve. The first to blink loses. Don't be afraid to put a buyer's offer off and encourage them to start with a better initial offer. Studies have shown that in the case of a $299,000 listing price, a buyer may start with an offer of $260,000. If you know your property isn't worth less than $275,000 or more than $299,000 encourage your buyer to give you his very best offer at the beginning of negotiations. The buyer should feel compelled to do this since you have told him indirectly that you have another party interested in the house. Since you haven't accepted any offers "yet," our magical three-letter word has created a sense of urgency in the buyer. A relaxed and encouraging tone in your voice should rather easily get the buyer up to a $270,000 or $280,000 starting offer. This extra-high starting point will yield you a higher net number since the last step in the negotiations will be to "split the difference" and meet in the middle (à la John Wayne). Splitting the difference at a higher starting point is the magical way to put thousands of extra dollars in your pocket. If the buyer does not feel that you're seriously entertaining another interested party, this won't work. It's not what you say; it's how you say it. We highly recommend you practice this technique with another person over the phone or in a mirror to perfect the technique.

These are the steps, which we highly recommend, that you should take in order to work your way smoothly into the rhythm of negotiating. Just like dancing, the last section covered the steps. The next section will cover the timing and the rhythm of the steps to be taken.

The Rhythm of the Negotiations

Negotiating has a certain rhythm to it that you should be aware of before you begin. Like dancing, you will need to keep a steady pace, not too fast or too slow, making sure you're in sync with your partner and not stepping on her toes. Respect the other person's space and remember how important it is that you never offend the buyer, her family, her broker, and especially the real estate maven. Disagreeing with the maven in front of the buyer or anyone else is not recommended because you'll alienate the person who has the buyer's confidence. For amateurs, negotiating the final price should probably be done over the phone in order to keep the conversation focused and one on one.

The day of the open house is when you are really going to get a feel for who's likely to open negotiations with you. As we discussed earlier, the re-show is the strongest indication of interest, second only to an actual offer. Using this knowledge, you can start preparing your foundation of negotiations at the re-show. It's absolutely a matter of going slow and taking your time.

Some sellers feel compelled to try and get prospects to sign on the dotted line too quickly. Our experience has shown that a common denominator has emerged as a prototype for the timing of negotiations. The buyers that ultimately buy tend to fall within to the following pattern. They see the house at the open house on a Sunday; they come back on Monday with their real estate maven; and on Monday night (after the kids are in bed) they call with an offer. The typical seller's temptation is to push too hard and try to agree on a price in the same conversation. This is the classical amateur mistake. Great fisherman all know that you don't yank the hook out of the fish's mouth the first time the fish goes near the bait. It's the nervous energy that normally dooms the seller by either talking excessively or by trying to agree on a price too quickly. Think of this process like a ballet instead of like break dancing.

If you are using a price range listing as we discussed in Chapter 5, a proper explanation to the buyer as to how it works is imperative. This must be done before the buyer gives you an offer. For example, if your price range listing is between $499,000 and $525,000, you need to tell the buyer that the minimum opening offer on the property must be $499,000 for you, the seller, to enter into negotiations with them. The typical dialogue that we have practiced successfully countless times with astoundingly positive results has been the following:

"Mr. Buyer, our price range listing is between $499,000 and $525,000. We require a minimum bid of $499,000 in order to enter into negotiations. We truly feel the property is worth no less than $500,000 and probably not more than $525,000, and since you the buyer are able to accommodate our terms (occupancy date and other qualifications), we feel that it is fair to settle on a price in the middle at $512,500."

This dialogue should occur in several steps. First, get the buyer to agree to an opening bid of $499,000. Second, ensure that the terms and other pertinent negotiating items are agreed upon first before the final step of meeting halfway at the middle point of the range of price. The biggest mistakes amateurs make occur because they are all fearful of underpricing their property and believe, mistakenly (especially in a down market), that they need to leave a significant amount of negotiating room for price so that the buyers can feel that they have received a great deal. As logical as this may seem, it is 100 percent counterproductive for achieving the highest possible price.

Insider Secret

Very well-seasoned real estate brokers have learned that even in the most dismal of real estate markets, slightly underpricing the house will produce the highest ultimate selling price. The price range listing should bracket the true value of the property by 5 percent over and 5 percent under the most likely selling price the property will yield. The lower price of the price range will lure in the buyers. The higher price of the range will give the buyers the necessary bragging rights to their family and friends.

Last, price range listings greater than an aggregate total range of more than 10 percent are simply too much.

What to Do When the Offer Is Presented

When the offer is presented by the buyers, it would probably be best to do as much listening as possible, speak the absolute least that you can, and let them know that tomorrow after lunch you'll be calling after you speak to your spouse (or your own maven). If you're using a listing broker, the offer may come via fax. Resist the temptation to respond by phone or fax for a full day. If you like, your broker can call the buyer's broker and say, "We've received your offer and will be getting back to you on Tuesday."

Tuesday

After lunch, call your buyers back as promised. If their offer is within your bracketed range of value, let them know how you really had listed your house at the price that you felt the house was really worth. Your buyers will agree, since the proof is in the pudding . . . you have an offer. It's critical to reiterate to them, slowly and clearly, perhaps several times, the listing price. It's almost as if you want to raise their sights at the higher mark before you agree to meet in the middle. It is an insidious temptation to all sellers to want to squeeze the buyer to a point more than the middle point between your asking price and their last offer. This is not the time to squeeze them. The *last* step in negotiations should be simple and courteous. We've lost hundreds of deals because of buyers' remorse. Surveying buyers after the fact has revealed that the number one reason buyers changed their mind and got remorseful was because they felt that they had not reached a fair price. If you want to squeeze the buyer, the time to do that is at the initial point of negotiations. Specifically, that is, by getting the buyer to their highest possible starting point. If you feel that the resulting midway point would not be acceptable to you, then you should simply decline the initial offer and ask them to resubmit.

The Ball Is in Their Court

If negotiating was a tennis match, each time the ball is hit, a day should pass. The major advantage of this is it gives the buyer and seller the time to digest each offer and counter. You may have overlooked discussing critical issues prior to accepting the final price. The devil is in the details—closing date, occupancy date, contingencies, earnest money deposit, down payment, financing terms, and so on. Remember, the price is the last thing to negotiate; if you agree on a price too early and you later need to make a concession on a key term of the transaction—which you should have handled earlier—it is almost impossible to get the buyer to come up in price once you've already agreed upon it. So think of the price as the icing on the cake. If the buyers want to taste the icing, they will simply have to wait until you've gone through your checklist of baking the cake.

Stop Talking When You Have the Sale

Have you ever been to a car dealer and had a salesman just run off at the mouth about the car after you've convinced yourself to buy it? In some cases, the salesman might say something you weren't even concerned with and actually talk you *out* of the deal!

Remember, God gave us two ears and one mouth for a reason—listen twice as much as you talk. When you've got the sale, stop talking! So many people destroy a perfectly good deal by saying too much when they should just stop talking and go to the next step, which is putting the deal in writing.

The Hungriest Fish Get Fed First

The mysterious phenomenon of the first offer rule prevails much more often than not, perhaps even as much as 80 percent to 90 percent of the time. This rule of thumb says that the first offer received by a seller, when a property is properly exposed and priced, will often be the best offer the seller receives. It's hard to believe that you won't get a better offer by simply waiting. However, studies have shown that the hungriest fish in the tank of available buyers will get to the property first because they are the most alert, the hungriest, and will take the biggest bite, hence the biggest offer. This analogy is really a metaphor for buyers watching for new homes that splash onto the market. The buyers who are most actively looking and the most ready to buy typically get to the property within the first three weeks of its being launched on the market. This is assuming, of course, that you have done your due diligence and you have priced it by following our instructions in this book and that you have properly presented the property.

The Double-Offer Conundrum

If you have done everything we have outlined, you may find yourself in the lucky conundrum of having more than one buyer chomping at the bit for your property. While this is a fortunate position to be in, the worst thing you want to do is blow it by working one buyer against the other and losing both. Having competing buyers is a delicate situation and must be handled properly in order to get the right buyer of the two closed, with the highest possible price. The likelihood of losing both buyers is much greater than you can possibly imagine. The fortune cookie says, "He who chases two rabbits, catches no rabbits."

So, how should you handle two simultaneous offers? We could write an entire book on this topic, but we'll give you the short and simple version. The principles we've discussed earlier should be implemented in the exactly same way with each buyer. When you tell them you haven't accepted any offers yet, you may clarify this one step further by saying, "You haven't signed a contract of sale yet." If you should decide that the second offer is the one you want to go with, the first offer must be handled delicately. If you tell the first buyer that you've decided to go with another buyer, it's extremely likely that if your second offer should fall through, your first buyer will have lost the love for your property. Once you have accepted the second buyer's offer, but haven't gotten the deal in writing yet, you want to keep your first buyer warm in case your second buyer falls through. We do not want to mislead our first buyer, but we will tell him that his current offer is simply not high enough. The point we're trying to make is that you don't want to break the first buyer's heart by telling him you've accepted another offer until after the second buyer has officially signed the contract of sale. Besides, if your second deal falls through when it is time to go back to the first deal, hard feelings won't be part of the equation.

The Close

In some cases the buyer will submit the offer in writing via their real estate agent, in which case you're already into the negotiating and closing phase. But, if you're dealing with the buyers face to face or by phone without their real estate broker, you may have to make the move to close the sale. At some point you'll have to nudge the buyer into the final decision to make the purchase, sign an agreement, and give up an earnest money deposit.

The dynamics may contain several variables, the most relevant of which is whether they are being represented by a broker. It has become common practice for the buyer's broker to draft the offer in the form of a purchase contract and submit it to the seller's listing agent by fax. If you're using a discount broker, then the offer will likely come straight to you. If your buyer is not being represented by an agent and neither are you, then you will be dealing face to face and drafting the contract on your own or having an attorney do it for you.

Putting It in the Contract

If you're listing the property through a real estate broker or the buyer has a broker who has submitted an offer, the contract will be drawn up by one of the brokers. Unless you live in a state where attorneys commonly draft the contract, you'll need to learn how to fill out a contract and get the buyer to sign on the dotted line. The following are the basic principles of real estate contracts. We recommend that you find a copy of the contract that brokers commonly use for real estate transactions and become familiar with how to properly fill in the blanks.

Basic Contract Principles

Real estate contracts are based on common contract principles, so it's important for you to understand the basics of contract law. The process begins with an offer. A contract is formed when an offer is made and accepted. In most states, standardized contracts drafted in the form of offers are used by real estate agents and attorneys. The offer is usually signed by the buyer (the offeror) and contains all the material terms of a contract, with the exception of the seller's signature.

The basic building block of a contract is mutual agreement. The contract isn't binding until the seller accepts, which creates a meeting of the minds. An acceptance is made if the offeree (the seller, in this case) agrees to the exact terms of the offer. If the offer comes back to the offeror with changes, there is no binding contract, but rather a counteroffer. Thus, if the seller signs the purchase contract, but changes the closing date to five days sooner, there is no agreement. Furthermore, if the offer isn't accepted within the time frame and manner set forth by the offeror, no contract is formed. For example, if the contract specifies that acceptance must be made by facsimile, an acceptance by telephone call or mail will not suffice.

Basic Legal Requirements of a Real Estate Contract

Several basic requirements must be present to make a real estate contract valid:

Mutual Agreement. As stated earlier, there must be a mutual agreement or a meeting of the minds.

In Writing. With few exceptions, a contract for purchase and sale of real estate must be in writing to be enforceable. Thus, if a buyer makes an offer in writing and the seller accepts orally but later backs out, the buyer is out of luck.

Identify the Parties. The contract must identify the parties. Although not legally required, a contract commonly sets forth full names and middle initials.

Identify the Property. The contract must identify the property. Though not required, a legal description should be included. A vague description such as "my lakefront home" may not be specific enough to create a binding contract.

Purchase Price. The contract must state the purchase price of the property or a reasonably ascertainable figure (such as "appraised value as determined by ABC Appraisers, Inc.").

Consideration. A contract must have consideration to be enforceable. Consideration is the benefit, interest, or value that induces a promise; it's the glue that binds a contract. The amount of consideration isn't important from a legal standpoint, but as a practical matter it will show how motivated the buyer is, and will commit him more emotionally to the deal if he has a more sizeable earnest-money deposit.

Earnest Money

A buyer will usually put up earnest money to bind the contract and show that he is a serious buyer. Most sellers ask for the earnest money deposit because they're afraid of tying up the property and rejecting other potential buyers.

How Much Earnest Money Is Necessary?   The law requires no specific amount of earnest money. In fact, a seller's promise to sell and a buyer's promise to buy are sufficient consideration to legally bind the parties to a contract. However, as a seller you should ask for 3 to 5 percent of the purchase price from the buyer. Collecting earnest money will give the buyer some skin in the game so he's less likely to back out before closing.

Contingencies

A contingency is a clause in a contract that must be satisfied for the contract to be complete. If the contingencies are not satisfied, the contract terminates, and the parties go their separate ways. The contract will usually provide that in the event of termination, the buyer is entitled to keep his earnest money.

Inspection Contingency. Most standard real estate contracts contain an inspection clause, which gives the buyer a certain amount of time to inspect the premises. After he inspects the premises, he should provide the seller with a list of potential problems or defects and give the seller a chance to remedy these problems, adjust the purchase price, or terminate the agreement. Most standard inspection clauses place the burden of inspecting and disapproving on the buyer. Thus, his failure to timely inspect and object will result in his waiver of this contingency. Used properly, the inspection clause will allow a buyer to terminate a contract that was signed hastily and later turns out to be a bad deal. If your buyer develops a case of buyer's remorse, he'll likely use the inspection contingency to back out of the contract.

As we discussed in Chapter 2, it's a good idea to get your property inspected before you offer it for sale—for two reasons. The first is to make sure there are no safety issues that could lead to liability stemming from an injury. The second is so that you can anticipate what possible objections a buyer will have when he inspects the property. Property inspections are typically done by a professional property inspector or, preferably, a licensed home inspector (if they are licensed in your state).

Keep in mind that the inspection contingency is often used by the buyer to reopen the negotiating process, even after the property is under contract. If the buyer's inspector comes up with a punch list of needed repairs, the buyer or his agent will try for further reductions of the price. These are known as "concessions." If you've already done your own inspection, you'll have headed off as many potential inspection issues as possible, but keep in mind that every inspector is human, so he sees things through a different perspective and may come up with his own list of needed repair items. It's a good idea to meet with the inspector at the property to try and mitigate what could be a poor inspection report. In some states like New York, home inspections are done before the contract of sale.

Loan Approval Contingency. Virtually every standard real estate contract gives the buyer a contingency to find a loan to purchase the property. The buyer is obligated to make reasonable efforts to make applications to various lenders and comply with the lenders' demands for proof of employment, copies of tax returns, and other documentation. The loan contingency will usually state a certain date by which the buyer must present the seller with a copy of a written loan commitment from the lender. If the deadline is not met, the seller can extend the deadline or the contract fails. If several weeks have gone by and there's been no appraisal done on the property, it typically means the loan process has not been moving along schedule. It is imperative to stay on top of this detail.

Marketable Title. The contract will usually provide that it is contingent upon proof of a marketable title by a certain date. Title to the property is "marketable" if the seller can deed it to the buyer at closing free and clear from all liens. Typically the seller will have a mortgage lien on the property, but will use the buyer's purchase money to pay off the existing mortgage lien at closing. The seller is usually required to provide the buyer a copy of a title report or a title commitment showing that the title is marketable and insurable by a title company.

It is imperative that title be ordered right away so that there is sufficient time to cure any title issues that may arise. We have seen countless transactions fall apart merely because the title was ordered too late in the process.

Signatures

A contract must be signed to be enforceable. The party signing must be of sound mind and of legal age—a contract signed by a minor younger than 18 is voidable. A notary's signature or witness isn't required. A facsimile signature is usually acceptable, as long as the contract states that facsimile signatures are valid.

Chapter Summary

- Negotiating is a delicate process that requires some learning and preparation.
- Listen much more than you speak.
- Consider whether you want to negotiate face to face or over the phone.
- Learn how to properly handle the first offer and multiple offers.
- Learn how to fill out a real estate contract form.

CHAPTER 10

It's Been Several Months and It Hasn't Sold— Try the Round-Robin Auction Method!

"Never, Never, Never, Never, Never give up."
  —Winston Churchill, Speech delivered at Harrow School,
October 29, 1941

If your house still hasn't sold and you're less concerned with price and more concerned with just getting rid of it, the round-robin auction may be the way to go to get a reasonable price for your house. A round-robin auction, which is sometimes referred to as a bid auction, can be one of the most powerful, exciting, rewarding, and fun experiences you'll ever have when going through the process of selling a home. The process was popularized about 15 years ago by Bill Effros in his book *How to Sell Your Home in Five Days* (Workman Publishing 1993). The auction method is unconventional, but can be effective.

The round-robin strategy isn't specifically for selling in a slow market. The technique will work in any market. Many people use this strategy when the market has slowed, but it works in a seller's market as well. The basic process involves marketing the property for at least 5 consecutive days and as many as 10, inviting people to a 2-day open house, then asking for bids at the end of the weekend. After the end of the weekend, you'll contact the bidders and try to get each to raise their bid to the highest amount they're willing to pay. The property is sold to the highest bidder, at which point you draft a regular sales contract. You can set a reserve amount, which is the minimum you're willing to accept in case you don't get any offers above what you're looking for as your bottom line. If you've ever used Internet auction sites (such as eBay.com), you'll have familiarity with how bidding works.

Benefits of the Round-Robin Auction

Why a Round-Robin Auction? Here are six reasons:

1. **Competitive environment.** The number one reason to do a round-robin auction is to create a competitive environment in which people are bidding against each other for your house. People often get caught up in the phenomenon of auction fever and end up paying more than they had planned. The more people you have bidding against each other, the better chance you'll have of getting a higher price.

2. **High Traffic.** The process of the round-robin creates a lot of traffic through your house because of the low initial price offering. Normally, a low price would invite people to either be scared away or try to beat you up even more. In this case, the low price invites people to bid *more* than the initial offering price, because they know others will be bidding against them. Also, the lower price attracts many more potential bidders because they think they're in for a bargain opportunity. Studies have shown that words such as "auction," "estate," and "foreclosure" often invite bargain hunters to get involved even if they don't pay a bargain price for the property.

   This strategy seems to work best when you have a healthy pool of buyers. It can be more difficult in rural areas with scant traffic. There just may not be enough of a demand in the rural areas to get a large group of buyers to your open house. It seems to work best in the cities and the suburbs. It really works best in the median-price neighborhoods. You can try this strategy in the luxury market, but you really need to cast a wide net to capture people who can afford and qualify to buy your house. Common sense tells us that it's much easier to market and sell a $250,000 house than a $1 million home or a $5 million home.

3. **Quick Sale.** The process takes about a week to implement and will generally yield a quick sale. The price won't necessarily be the highest price, but you'll sell it quickly and for the highest reasonable price considering the time frame. If you don't want to deal with a long selling process, the auction will get things done quickly so that you can get on with your life.

4. **Only One Weekend.** Let's face it; keeping your home in tip-top shape is a pain in the neck. The round-robin auction open house lasts only two days, so there's less to worry about. Instead of having to keep your house ready for showings 24/7 for months at a time, you'll get it done in a weekend, so you can get your house in perfect shape for just a short time, rather than keeping it in pretty good shape for months.

5. **Modest Marketing Budget.** In terms of bang for your buck, the round-robin is relatively cheap to implement and can be done without a listing broker, leaving more room for profit in your pocket (or room for you to cut the price to get it sold quickly).

6. **Gathering a Long List of Buyers.** Even if you don't get an acceptable bid for your home, the fact that you've gotten a list of a few hundred names of people who are interested in purchasing a home in this neighborhood is something that has tremendous value. Even if you don't get the bid you want, you're doing a killer open house. This is a great tactic for real estate investors and real estate professionals.

Your First Consideration—Your Equity

As you consider how to implement the auction strategy you need to first evaluate your mortgage situation. Do you own your property free and clear of any liens? Do you have equity in your home, or is the house fully leveraged? Do you need all cash or would you be willing to accept owner financing on all or some of the purchase price? The answers to these questions will help you to decide how to approach selling your home and whether to get it done quickly using the auction method. Of course, the more equity you have in your home the more flexible you can be and the more choices you have available. For those of you who have little or no equity your options are limited with this technique, unless you can negotiate a short sale with your lender.

Picking the Right Weekend

As we discussed in Chapter 8, picking the right weekend is crucial to your initial exposure to your house. The same rules apply for the round-robin auction. Avoid big events like Super Bowl weekend, Memorial Day, or other three-day weekends when people typically leave town. Check your calendar, and plan accordingly. You'll want to give yourself at least two weeks lead time. You're going to need about a week to execute the plan once everything is in place.

Initially, you'll need to decide whether to use the auction method before using the traditional sales method or whether you will try the traditional route first, but then use the auction method as a last ditch attempt. This will depend on whether getting top dollar is your first priority. If so, then marketing the property for a few months using the traditional method first is probably the better way to go in most cases. If you offer the property via auction as your first exposure to the market, you'll have already offered a low price, and it will be hard to raise the price.

Doing the Legwork

If you haven't already done so, order an appraisal and any inspections or reports that a potential buyer would want to see. There will be a lot of people coming to your open house, and you're asking them to make a commitment to buy your house in one weekend. The more information you can give them as far as comparable sales in the area, market value, home inspection results and possible home warranty, pest inspection, and so forth, the easier you'll make it for them to make a decision to buy your home. Taking care of these matters also gives you an edge on your competition because most people don't go the extra mile when it comes to preparation and attention to detail. Do everything for your potential buyers that you would want a seller to do for you in the same situation. You'll want to make it easy for them to buy.

Now that you've selected a weekend for your auction, you'll have to get your home ready to show. If you've followed the techniques in Chapter 4, your house should be in tip-top shape and ready to go to market. One of the great advantages of doing a round-robin auction and selling your home in one weekend is that you only have to prepare your home once and keep it in perfect shape for just that one weekend. Otherwise, you'll have to maintain both the yard and the inside of the home every single day because you never know when someone will be stopping by to have a showing. This can take several months or more. You may even have several open houses, and this in itself can be stressful.

If you're living in the same house that you're trying to sell, it's extremely difficult to keep the house ready to show at a moment's notice. It's just not practical or realistic. And if you're following the recommendation we made to put many of your possessions in storage to remove the clutter and make your home appear more spacious, you'll need to factor in the expense of storage fees. It's much better to pay for one month of storage and be done with it than to pay for six to nine months of storage and be denied the use and access to the things you normally have in your home. By using the auction strategy you'll work hard for a short period of time. After you show the house for the two-day weekend you've chosen for your auction, it's over. You'll end up with a better deal and a lot less stress, and you can get on with your life sooner.

What's Your Bottom Line?

Next, you'll want to identify your bottom-line price for the sale of your house. Ask yourself these questions: "If I sold my home this weekend to a cash buyer, what is my bottom-line acceptable price?" In other words, ask yourself, "If I can't get this price, then will I keep the house? After it's all said and done, what would I be happy netting on this sale? If I can't get this price, then I'm going to continue to market my house the traditional way."

If you're in a slow-moving market, don't rely on getting more than 85 to 90 percent of today's appraised value of your home. You certainly could get more, but don't rely on it. Consider this: if you sell a house through a broker, offer a seller discount, and deduct for repairs and holding costs, sometimes you'll be lucky to net 85 to 90 cents on the dollar. It might cost you 10 to 15 percent in holding and transaction costs. It's not unreasonable or unusual for sellers to accept a 5 percent discount on their property in order to facilitate a quicker sale. And most, real estate commissions are 6 percent of the sales price if an agent is used by both the buyer and the seller. This adds up to 11 percent off the asking price already. Most sellers incur these costs. So getting an offer of 85 percent to 90 percent to buy your home now rather than six months from now is a solid offer and one most sellers should consider taking.

If you're selling your house yourself, you can avoid some of these costs. If you're happy taking 85 to 90 cents on the dollar, then the auction strategy is a great strategy for you to use. If you must get more than that, then you may not want to do an all-cash auction. Remember, an all-cash auction is only one type of auction and is a strategy designed for people in a specific situation and set of circumstances. For those of you who must have more than 85 to 90 cents on the dollar, consider the owner financing route. And just to clarify, when we say 85 cents on the dollar we mean 85 percent of the current *appraised* value of the home.

Remember that there's a certain value in selling now versus carrying the property and having to drop the price. As we discussed in Chapter 9, what a lot of people do is price their home extremely high just to see what kind of initial offers they'll get. Then, when they don't get any offers, they're forced to drop their price. They have to keep dropping it and dropping it, and then after a while people start to wonder why the property has been on the market for so long. They start to think that something must be wrong with the property. Then the sellers have to drop the price so low that they end up losing money. They taint the property by playing that game.

You can advertise the appraised value of the home, but you want to advertise the opening bid at about 70 percent of the appraised value. Let's use an example of a $300,000 house. You would ask for an opening bid of $210,000. You're advertising that you will be selling your home in one weekend and by Sunday night you'll sell it to the person whose bid is the "highest reasonable offer." This is the key phrase. An important point to understand is that even though you're selling it for the highest reasonable offer, you should set a "reserve" price in your mind. Your reserve price might be that 85 cents on the dollar we spoke of earlier. The reserve price is the price at which you won't accept anything lower. It's the minimum price that you have decided you would accept. Any bids below this will be considered unreasonable, and you won't accept them. You disclose to everyone who comes to the auction that the house will be sold to the person with the "highest reasonable offer," the opening bid is $210,000 and if you don't get a reasonable offer you won't sell the house. You have a reserve sales price in mind, but you don't disclose it to the people who attend the auction.

Create an Informational Packet

One of the most important things you'll have to do is prepare informational materials, sometimes called a buyer's kit, for the people attending your auction. We feel that two of the most important items you can include in this packet are a recent appraisal and a home inspection report by a certified home-inspection service.

Your comp book is especially helpful because it contains information about your competition and the neighborhood. Include as much information as you can in your information packet, such as the following:

- Information about the property (such as color picture brochure and a survey)
- Inspection report
- Appraisal and/or recent comps
- Information about the schools
- Information about warranties
- Information about the homeowners' association and covenants, conditions, and restrictions (CC&Rs)
- Information about taxes and insurance
- Copy of the deed
- Terms of the auction (including the fact that there is a reserve)
- Answers to frequently asked questions

You may even want to include color photos and have the information packet nicely bound with a spiral binding. Kinko's is very helpful for creating these information packets. You'll probably want a few hundred ready for the auction open house.

Marketing For the Auction

The reality of this whole strategy is that if you perform well on your marketing campaign and you attract a lot of people to your one open house, the market will dictate what the house is worth. The appraisal may say one thing, but remember that a house is only worth what somebody is willing to pay for it. You are letting the free market determine the value of your home.

Marketing should begin about five to ten days prior to your open house.

Signs, Signs, Everywhere There's Signs

Signs will give you a tremendous bang for your buck. You'll first want to place a large sign in front of the home that looks something like this:

In addition, you'll want to place directional signs around the neighborhood that look similar, such as the following:

Newspaper Ads

Advertise small display ads in the newspaper from Monday through Sunday, using similar language as in the signs. A phone number and web site should be placed in the ad for maximum response.

7 DAY HOME AUCTION

House sold to the highest reasonable bidder.
175 Maple Lane – Open Inspection Sat/Sun

Go to **www.175maplelane.com** for details
Or call (343)-333-4873 for details

Web Sites

Web sites such as Craigslist are extremely effective for advertising a home auction. The trick to using the site (www.craigslist.org) is to keep re-posting the advertisement every day (twice a day on weekends) to keep it at the top. Make sure you include a link to your web site for the property, which should contain information about the property and the auction process.

Human-Spinner Signs

If you live in area with new home construction, you've no doubt seen a young kid with a large, directional sign spinning it around and pointing in the direction of the homes. On the days of the open-house inspection period, hire a neighbor's kid or someone from craigslist.org to stand on the nearest street corner with a sign.

Mailers

Mail flyers and postcards to everyone in your neighborhood and within a one-mile radius. Turn to the Internet (www.printing-forless.com and www.vistaprint.com) for reasonable prices on short-run color jobs.

The Open House

Once you've marketed the property for five to seven days, you'll be ready for the "inspection period," which is a fancy name for the open house. You'll have a bid sheet at the house where people can write down their offers. You'll want as many people to show up during the specified time period as possible, so they can all see that there's considerable competition and demand for the house being auctioned. They start thinking that this must be a good house and a good deal, because they're seeing that there's a great deal of demand for it. People get excited and emotional, and that's exactly the mindset you're trying to foster. It can create a feeding frenzy and that psychology of the auction atmosphere and the competition is exactly what you want.

You want a couple of families to fall in love with the house, and then the price becomes secondary because they already want the house on an emotional level. Not everyone who comes to the auction will make you a reasonable offer. If you're selling a $300,000 home for $210,000, you're going to attract all kinds of people with many different motives. You'll have people who are looking for a home to move into and raise their family, speculators and investors thinking they can steal the house, and real estate professionals checking out the competition in their area and possibly trying to get the listing on your house at the same time. But all of these people add to the number of attendees and help to create the emotional atmosphere you're striving for. To boost your numbers, invite friends, family, and neighbors if you have to, but make sure the open house looks as busy as possible. Just offer free food, and you'll have no problem filling up your house!

Open Bidding

Each person must write his name and bid price on the sheet (see Appendix H for a sample). It's not a closed or secret bid. Each person can see what others have bid. Make a special point to tell all bidders to at least submit a bid no matter what it may be. Tell them that if they want to remain in the bidding and would like you to call them Sunday night, they can just put anything down as a bid. If they do that, then they are still part of the process. You'll call them

Sunday night at the conclusion of the open house and auction, and they'll be given another opportunity to make a higher bid and continue to be contacted in the bidding process until they either make the highest bid or drop out. Once you have a high bidder you're satisfied with, enter into a regular purchase contract, and close like a conventional sale.

As we discussed in Chapter 8, you'll also want to provide a sign-in sheet with a raffle of some kind so that you get *all* the names of people who attend the open house. Remember, the point of the auction is not just to sell the house on the spot but also to get as many potential buyers through the house, so you can follow up with them and then get the house sold.

The Auction Is Over, Now What?

At the end of two days (on Sunday night or Monday morning), peruse your list, so you can call people on the bid sheet. Call your highest bidder first. Here's what you will say. Tell them they're the highest bidder and congratulate them. Then you tell them that if they want, they can preempt their own bid. That means that they can raise their bid now. This may cause more people to drop out during the first round, and they'll have less competition. Do not pressure them to up their bid. Let them know in a comfortable way that it's totally up to them as an option. They can keep their bid as is, or they can up their initial bid. Tell them you can call everybody else on the list and come back to them, or they can raise their bid at that moment.

What usually happens is all the people who aren't serious drop out in the first round. Once you've gone through the list and called everyone, then start over again by calling all the bidder's and giving them a chance to increase their bid. Now you're beginning the second round of the round-robin auction and you go through the process all over again. You continue to follow this process until you have a winning bidder.

We referred earlier to an information packet that you'll prepare for each of the attendees. You want to include the bidding instructions as part of this package so that everyone knows exactly how the process works, what to expect, and how to make sure they remain in the running for the purchase of the home come Sunday night when you begin calling. You'll probably end up with one bid right behind the highest bidder, and you may have a third bidder just behind the second-highest bidder.

Ask each bidder to raise their bid in increments of $1,000. This is the minimum they can increase their bid. If there are multiple bidders, tell them to raise it $5,000, even though in the bidding instructions it will say $1,000. This way you won't have two or more bidders at the same bid price. Two people could have different bids, but you should consider the highest bidder the one who will give you the highest net price. Now, if we end up with the same net price for two different bidders and one of them is using an agent, then I'll usually choose the buyer who isn't using the agent to keep things simple.

Getting It In Writing

On Monday, call and congratulate the highest bidder, and set up an appointment to meet so you can proceed to getting the sale of your house or property under contract. By the time you make all your calls on Sunday night, it will be late in the evening, so you want to do this as soon as possible on Monday. Up to this point all you really have is a verbal commitment to purchase your home, so you want to get things down in writing immediately.

Assuming your second-highest bidder has also made a reasonable offer, you contact them and tell them that you want to meet with them and put them under a backup contract as well so they'll be in the back-up position. (A backup contract is one that is contingent on another contract falling through.) You tell them that if the first contract should fall apart for any reason they'll be in a position to move forward with their purchase of the house. It's important to get them under contract. By doing so you have given them hope that they still may have a chance to buy your home. If you don't get them under contract, they'll continue to look at properties, and they may find another home by the time you call and tell them that the first contract fell through. However, if they're under contract with you and they feel they have a reasonable chance to buy your home, then they may stop looking at other properties for at least the next two to three weeks. This will give you adequate time to find out if your first buyer is a qualified buyer or not and if you in fact need your back-up buyer to perform.

Closing the Transaction

The fact that you've sold your house by using the round-robin auction strategy has nothing to do with the type of closing that will take place. The closing is just a normal closing. Some people prefer to call it a "retail" closing. The buyer usually follows up with a lender to secure a loan on the property. With financing in place, the closing progresses to a satisfactory conclusion. If the buyers do not qualify for a loan, then they're not committed to buying the house. You'll usually know within a matter of a few weeks if your buyer is qualified or not. If your buyer doesn't qualify, then you immediately call the second buyer and say that the first buyer is not able to finalize the purchase of the home and that they can now begin the process of buying the home themselves. Remember, you had put them under contract at the conclusion of the auction to be prepared for this situation. This is why, it's always important to have at least one back-up contract. Assuming that the second and third bidders have also submitted reasonable offers, it's better to have these as back-up offers, too.

Frequently Asked Questions

What If the Buyer Has an Agent?

Many buyers work with an agent who is trying to find them a house (buyer's agent). If this is the case, you can simply pay the agent her commission (generally 3 percent) from the sales price of the house. However, when you're comparing two bids at the same price you must consider the net profit you'll receive. For example: if you have two bids at $300,000 and one bid uses an agent while the other does not, you might accept the bid where a real estate professional is not involved because you'll net more on your bottom line. The bid price is the same, but you would have to pay approximately $9,000 in commissions that will chip away considerably from your net profit on the house. You're looking for the best net price on the bid. The person who offered you the $300,000 without agent involvement is actually the highest bidder when you consider the overall net price you would receive.

You should avoid telling people that they can't use an agent because it will discourage them from making a bid. Many people feel more comfortable with an agent assisting them because they trust the agent to make sure that the contract and paperwork are done properly. Most people are not willing to write contracts and go through the entire home-buying process without the assistance of a professional. Remember, your goal is to get as many people to the open house auction as possible. So you must make everyone welcome. Don't discourage anyone from participating.

Why Only Two Days?

The number of hours and the number of days you decide to be open for your open house and to accept bids is totally up to you. If you only open it up for one day, you may get too many people and not have enough time for each person to thoroughly look at the house. Also, some people may not be able to make it one day or another. Also, someone coming in on Saturday may want to come back and have a second look on Sunday. Two days is an effective time period to work within. Some people have also reported that doing two separate weekends works well, too, but this may result in less of a deadline, which discourages the urgency mode that people go into it with a short deadline. On the other hand, if getting a lot of traffic through the house is your ultimate goal rather than selling it within a week, you may just use the auction method as a ruse to get people through the house in the hope that someone might just fall in love with it and pay you an acceptable price.

Why All Cash?

While the bidding method for all cash works as a bidding price very well, you can certainly accepts bids with owner financing. In this case, your bid sheet should ask for the total price, amount of down payment buyers can afford and monthly payments they can afford. In the case of owner financing, you'll want to check the credit and qualifications of the buyer so that the high bid would be subject to approval. If the high bidder does not work out, you go to the next bidder and so on.

Do They Need to See the Home to Bid?

Some people will bid without seeing the home, which generally means they're just testing the waters to see how low an offer you'll accept. These aren't serious buyers, and you shouldn't accept offers from them. Some people will push you hard to see the home prior to the open house, but that sword can cut you two ways. On the one hand, if they're serious and will make you a good offer, you don't want to turn them away. On the other hand, if they're extra eager to see your home, they'll wait until the open house and make a bid, which could be even higher than you expect because they're afraid someone else will get the home. Ideally, you should only let buyers see the home during the inspection period and not before. If someone absolutely insists on seeing the property and seems sincere, you can exercise judgment on whether to make an exception. If someone wants a re-show before upping the ante, you can certainly show them the house privately after the initial inspection period.

What If Nobody Bids High Enough?

Remember, you have a reserve price for the property, which is the minimum you'll accept. Thus, this isn't the same as an absolute auction where the highest bidder is the winner. You're advertising that you will accept the highest *reasonable* offer, which is determined by you in advance. If you don't get the bid that you want, simply reject the bids or invite the people for a re-showing of the property so that you can convince them to raise their offer. There's always the possibility that you're off with your value asking price, in which case you'll need to go back to the comps to double-check that your pricing is in the right range.

Chapter Summary

- The auction method is an unconventional yet effective way to get a quick sale for a reasonable price.
- The auction will drive a lot of traffic through your door and produce a list of possible candidates to buy the home.

CHAPTER 11

Help, My House Is Worth Less than I Owe!

If I owe you a pound, I have a problem; but if I owe you a million, the problem is yours.

—John Maynard Keynes

Many people are caught in the pickle of owning a house worth less than what is owed on it. In this case, dropping the price to meet the market conditions means they have to come to closing with cash to make up the difference between the sales price and the balance owed on their mortgage. For people who are financially strapped, this isn't a viable option. A short sale is a possible way out for people in this situation.

A "short sale" occurs when the lender takes less than what is owed on the property in lieu of the full amount. Typically a short sale is done when the homeowner is in foreclosure or at least behind in payments, although some lenders will accept a short sale in markets where property values have substantially declined and the property is "upside down" on equity.

To accomplish a short sale, you need to convince your lender of three things:

1. The property is not worth what's owed on it.

2. You can't make the payments.

3. You are essentially insolvent.

If you have a property that is upside down but have other assets and substantial income, your lender will probably not be willing to accept a short sale on the property. The logic is that if you do have the means to pay but are just not willing to do so, the lender is not exactly thrilled about taking the hit on the debt owed. On the other hand, if you are up to your ears in debt with the property and are considering walking away from it anyway, you are a good candidate for a short sale. Walking away from a property means the lender will foreclose, and your credit will be ruined. Furthermore, if the foreclosure auction yields less than the lender is owed, the bank could sue you for the difference between what is owed and what the foreclosure auction yields, which is called a "deficiency." A deficiency is generally pursued in a separate lawsuit by the lender, which ends up in a court judgment that is valid for 10 years or more. The good news is that lenders don't routinely seek a deficiency judgment and try to collect because the efforts are usually fruitless. And, if you file for Chapter 7 bankruptcy, it will generally wipe out your liability for a deficiency.

Why Would a Lender Accept a Short Sale?

You may wonder why a lender would accept a short sale on the property for less than it is owed. Consider the lender's position—with a record number of defaults, lenders are in a tough position nationwide. The last thing it needs is another foreclosure to deal with. Secondly, the lender loses money by foreclosing a property, even if there was equity. Attorneys fees, lost opportunity cost, broker fees, and damage to the property all add up to lost revenue for the lender. And with a declining housing market in many areas of the country, the property will be worth even less by the time the foreclosure is finished, which can take up to a year in some states. In other words, lenders like short sales because it allows them to cut their losses early and solve a problem. It's a win-win scenario for the lender and the homeowner.

How to Approach a Short Sale

In order for the lender to accept a short sale, the homeowner must have an offer on the table. For example, if $250,000 is owed on the property, the homeowner must submit a copy of a written contract where someone is willing to pay say $225,000 for the property. The contract is written subject to the lender's approval of the short sale, which means in order to close, the lender must be willing to accept $225,000 in lieu of the full amount owed. Thus, if the lender does not approve the short sale, the contract is cancelled.

The contract is presented to the lender with the following information:

- *Comparable sales*, a broker's price opinion (BPO) or appraisal showing the value of the property. In most cases the lender will do its own appraisal or BPO on the property, but if you have a recent appraisal or BPO showing that the value of the property has dropped since the loan was originated, this will be helpful to your case.

- *Financial information of the borrower*, such as tax returns, W-2 income verification, bank statements, and a financial statement of assets and liabilities. You will want to submit as much information to the lender as possible showing that you are essentially insolvent and broke. Remember, your case to the lender is not that you don't want to pay the loan but rather that you are unable to pay.

- *A letter of hardship* written by the homeowner as to why they can't make the payments on the property. Write a letter in your own handwriting as to why you are in a precarious financial situation. For example, you might write that you have lost your job, received a pay cut, or been divorced. One or two pages summarizing why you are in financial trouble and can't make the payments will suffice.

- *A preliminary settlement statement* (form HUD-1) showing a workup of the transaction. This can be prepared by a title company or real estate broker.

The key to making the transaction work is to show the lender that the seller won't receive any money at closing. The settlement statement must reflect a zero-net amount due to the seller, otherwise the lender will balk. Think about it from their standpoint—why should they take a loss if the seller walks away with cash from closing?

Once the information is submitted to the lender, it will do either a BPO or appraisal on the property. Then, it will negotiate the amount of discount it will accept. If the BPO or appraisal comes in high, it will be very difficult to negotiate a short sale. For example, if the seller owes $250,000 and the appraisal comes in at $300,000, it is very unlikely the lender will accept $225,000. On the other hand, if the appraisal comes in at $240,000, it's likely it will accept $225,000. There's no magic formula, but lenders will generally accept somewhere between 80 and 90 percent of the appraised value or broker's opinion of value. If the loan is insured by the Federal Housing Administration (FHA), the maximum discount the lender will accept is 82 percent.

Pitfalls of a Short Sale

There are several pitfalls for the homeowner who does a short sale on his property with the lender. First, understand if the debt is not settled in "full satisfaction" of the entire loan, the lender reserves the right to sue you for a deficiency. In most states, the lender can obtain a deficiency judgment and go after you for the debt for a long time. On the other hand, if the short sale is in full satisfaction of the entire debt, then the debt that has been forgiven is considered a taxable gain and the lender will send you an Internal Revenue Service Form 1099 for the amount of the forgiven debt, which will be considered income reportable on your next tax return.

There are two ways to deal with this "phantom income" issue. If the property was your primary residence; the Mortgage Forgiveness Debt Relief Act of 2007 would come into play. Under this act, any such forgiveness of debt would not be treated as income so long as the property was your principal residence and the debt that was forgiven was "acquisition indebtedness" (the amount you originally borrowed, when you bought the property). So, if the property you did the short sale on was a rental or you moved out beforehand, the forgiveness of debt would be considered income.

A second way to deal with the forgiveness of debt is to file IRS Form 982, requesting that the debt relief not be treated as income. Essentially, you're pleading to the IRS that you were insolvent at the time of the debt relief, and therefore the relief should not be treated as income. If you file for bankruptcy protection, this shouldn't be hard to prove. We recommend that you review the matter with your attorney or tax advisor before proceeding with the short sale route.

What if the Lender Won't Play Ball

Unfortunately, lenders won't always accept a short sale, either because they believe the property is worth more or because they think they will net more money by foreclosing the property and reselling it on the open market. While not always logical, lenders sometimes act in ways that are not in their best interest, at least from your viewpoint. In this case you may be stuck with a property upside down and no buyers, in which case you have three options.

Option One—Come to Closing with Cash

If you owe just a little more than the house is worth and you have some cash, it may make sense to just come to closing with money and pay off the negative balance of the loan. Remember, if you don't sell the property, you are making payments every month on a place you don't want to live in or can't afford. It may make sense financially to bite the bullet and just pay off the difference. If you have money in your IRA or SEP, it may make sense to take it out to pay the difference owed, even if you receive a penalty from the IRS for doing so. Borrowing from a credit card cash advance or a relative are also options. Remember, if the property goes to foreclosure, your credit will be ruined for a long time, which will cost you more for everything you do—loans, insurance, even a job. Many employers will do credit checks on potential employees for a job involving handling money and may reject you if your credit is bad.

Option Two: Wait it Out

If you are not in a rush to move, you can wait out the market for another year to two until prices rebound. If prices slide even more, wait a few months and try a short sale with your lender again. If you can show several properties in your neighborhood that have sold for a lower price, you may be able to convince the lender to do a short sale the second time around.

If you are behind in payments and in a loan you cannot afford, try to negotiate a forbearance agreement with your lender. A forbearance is where you get the lender to agree to lower your monthly payments and add the back payments you owe onto the balance of the loan. If your payment is lowered, then the difference between what you should be paying and what you agree to pay is also added to the principal balance of the loan. In some cases you can get the lender to completely rework the loan into a new loan with a different interest rate or at least a fixed rate payment so you aren't burdened by rising payments on the loan if the market interest rates rise. Many lenders are open to reworking a loan these days simply because they don't want to take the property back. In many cases they'd rather rework the loan than take a 10 to 20 percent discount on what they are owed, as in the case of a short sale.

Option Three: Walk Away

Your third option is to simply walk away from the house and let it go into foreclosure. Nobody is going to arrest you for walking away from your obligation, but there are two consequences: (1) Your credit will be ruined for several years, and (2) the lender can seek a deficiency judgment. In some states a deficiency judgment is prohibited by a lender if the house is your principal residence. If not, and the lender goes after you for the debt, you can file for Chapter 7 bankruptcy or even work out a monthly payment plan with the lender for the balance owed. If this is the case, it is recommended that you consult with an attorney about your rights and responsibilities under your state law.

As a final note, if you decide you are going to walk away from the property and don't want to file for bankruptcy, ask the lender if it would consider a deed in lieu of foreclosure. A deed in lieu is when you deed your property back to the lender in exchange for their promise not to sue you for a deficiency. A deed in lieu has the same effect of ruining your credit as a foreclosure; however, you remove the risk of a lender deficiency judgment.

Chapter Summary

- If you owe more than your house is worth, consider a lender short sale.

- In order to do a short sale you must convince the lender that the property has declined in value.

- If you can't work a short sale, consider a forbearance agreement or reworking of the loan.

CHAPTER 12

Review and Action Plan

"Action is the antidote to despair."

—Joan Baez

Now that we've been through the entire process of selling your house quickly in a slow market, this chapter will review the process and give you a checklist and action plan. There are dozens of nuggets you can use whether you're selling your own house or you're a real estate broker trying to sell many houses.

A DOCTOR'S Advice

The principles of this book can be summarized in the acronym, "ADOCTORS," as in the solution to selling in a sick market. Another way to think of this book is as a doctoral degree that gives you information for selling a house quickly and for the highest possible price. Use ADOCTORS as a checklist as you go to make sure you're on the right track. When you feel you're off track, go back to the checklist and make sure you're doing following the process in a logical order. It's like having the digits of a phone number; you need them in the right order for the call to get through.

Attitude

In Chapter 1, we discussed your attitude, the most important step of beginning the sales process. You need to get your head in the right place to make the principles of this book work for you, which means you have to have belief and faith in your own ability to sell your house fast and for top dollar, even if the market isn't cooperating with you. A positive, can-do attitude is a must for beginning your journey; otherwise all of your attempts to sell your house will be half-hearted and ineffectual. You must be willing to commit no less than 100 percent for this to work for you.

Remember, it's a numbers game. That means you're looking for at least 100 prospective buyers to consider your house before you can get 10 real lookers and 1 qualified RAW (ready, able and willing) buyer to make you an offer. If you play the numbers game correctly, your highest and best user will likely be the one making the best offer in terms of price. If you limit yourself in terms of how much money it's costing you to fix up or market your property, your head is in the wrong place. Like baseball, you have to get up to the plate and swing at a lot of pitches before you get a hit. You also need several hits to score a run. The more times you get out there and swing, the more hits you'll get on your property and eventually increase your odds for a home run.

Due Diligence

Once your mindset is correct, you need to research the neighborhood and your market to make sure you're properly positioning your property in terms of looks, price, and terms. You will want to hire an appraiser and/or a good real estate broker to help you get access to good information about the neighborhood's comparable sales and listed properties. This process cannot be taken lightly or done half-heartedly, since your entire pricing and negotiating process lives or dies with the information you have researched about your market and your comps.

Organize Your Information and Your House

Once you've done your due diligence and gathered information, you need to organize it and get it ready for using it when you put your house on the market. You'll have to be prepared when you get questions about the property or the neighborhood. Delivering accurate information will raise your bar when dealing with prospective buyers.

You also need to get your house organized and in tip-top shape. Learning the right things to renovate so your house is marketable and similar to others in the same price range gives you added punch. Going the extra step and staging it will be the edge you have over the other properties, because you'll give buyers an unforgettable experience.

Customers

Customers, or potential customers, drive the sale. You can advertise your property the traditional way, but this will bring in only so many leads. You have to take an active role and go out and get your customers. To use a fishing analogy, you can stick out a line with a worm, or you can go to where you think the fish are located and drop out a large net. If you don't know where to fish and just drop a line out anywhere, who knows what you will catch? If you want to catch the right fish, you need to use the right bait, know the right time to fish, and, most important, find out where this particular kind of fish likes to swim. Once the fish bites, you'll have to learn how to keep him on your hook.

And, on the topic of getting customers, you will decide whether to try and sell it on your own, with a discount broker, or with a full-service broker. We generally recommend trying the first two for a few weekends, then finding the top broker to work with. Read over the section of Chapter 6 about how to find the best broker to help sell your house.

Terms

You'll have to decide which price and terms you'll be offering on the property. Most people offer only all-cash terms, which means the single deal point is price. If you're selling the house in a cash transaction, then you need to learn how to price it just right in the range of competition in your geographical area. The giggle and the no-brainer tests will help you hone your price down to the best price range and the most effective price for selling your house fast and at the best possible number.

The easier you can make it for a buyer to qualify for financing and get into your house, the broader the pool of interested buyers you'll create. Offering owner financing or a lease/option will increase your potential pool of buyers and, when you have one, will make it easier for him to get financed to purchase the property.

Open House

The marketing is all about bringing customers to your door for an open house. How you advertise and prepare for the open house is critical to your success in getting the highest and best buyer to show up and possibly make you an offer. Handling all of the leads in an effective way will allow you to know all the people who came and how to get in touch with them for a follow up. Most sellers simply let buyers walk in and out of the house without so much as getting their names. A more effective way is to raffle something off as a way to capture the information of all of your prospective buyers.

The way you handle prospective buyers as they walk through the house is crucial as well, starting with the most important features, sometimes even the outside first and ending up in the kitchen, the best place to discuss the deal. Remember to let the prospective buyers lead the way, and don't talk too much so that you distract them from the task at hand, which is trying on your house for size.

Round-Robin Auction

If your first attempts to sell the property on your own by using open houses and the multiple listing service do not succeed, the round-robin auction can be a very effective tool as a last-ditch attempt. While this method will not necessarily yield the highest price, it will get you a fair and reasonable price for the home and sell it within a weekend. At the very least, you will gather a number of leads for good, qualified prospects to follow up on who may be interested in purchasing it outside the auction process.

Say the Right Things

Learning how to say the right things to your prospective buyers is what separates showing the house and selling the house. The negotiating gambits we've discussed in this book are based on years of experience and thousands of successful transactions.

So there you have it, ADOCTORS advice for selling a house in a sick market. Use this acronym as your checklist and constantly refer to it so that you can make sure you are on track when selling your house.

Action Plan

Now that you have a checklist for what to do and in what order, you need to develop an action plan. The following is a good example of an organized action plan. Break it down by week and by day so that you have something to do every day. In order to keep your mind in the right place, which is positive and moving forward, you need to have something always to do on your task list. Software programs like Microsoft Outlook help to organize your day and week, although a good old-fashioned day planner or pocket notebook will do just fine.

Week One: Due Diligence and Organize Documentation

The first week you should prepare your information and find the key sources from which to get it. Hiring an appraiser or a real estate broker to act as a facilitator are the two best place to start. The next step is to map out your information in a logical fashion. If your comps book has been organized as we discussed in Chapter 5, then you may want to consider driving by the comps in the same logical fashion. Specifically, starting with the sold and under-contract properties first would be a good place to start. Get a laminated Hagstrom map and a dry-erase, fine-tipped pen, and underline the names of the streets in which your comps are located. Write the actual number of the address near the underlined mark of the street and circle that number.

Once you have mapped the locations (using Mapquest.com or a GPS system), you will have a bird's eye view and a relative perspective on how your subject property compares by location with your competitors within your defined geography. The advantage here is twofold. First, you will have an efficient method for driving by the properties. We recommend starting from the point furthest from your property and working your way home. Second, this will give you an opportunity to name the properties as we discussed in Chapter 5, so you will have an efficient system for recalling information about these properties. This is very helpful when speaking with prospective buyers, bank appraisers, home inspectors, and the buyer's real estate maven. The person with the greatest specific knowledge about the relative comps is usually the one who is regarded as the true expert in the negotiations. We recommend not viewing more than 5 to 10 properties using the drive-by method in one particular session. Try to break it up for a maximum of two sessions a day so you can finish the task within the first week.

The second map and drive-by session should be relative to the properties currently for sale. This map is, in a soft market, the most important part of your research because it is your most direct competition. It is highly recommended that you take twice as much time to study these comps. Plan to do this part of your research in two pieces. The first should be strictly the drive-by inspection, during which you will attempt to judge the relative price of the property as compared to your subject property. The second part of your research would be to actually go to the open houses and look at the inside of these properties. If you cannot make the open house or there is no open house in your time period, then call the listing broker to get a showing of the property. If you are not comfortable doing this, then at least try to get a look at the pictures on the MLS web site, flyer, or seller's web site. At the very least, you want to get an inside inspection of your two closest competitors.

Once you are done with your research about sold, under-contract, and for-sale properties, you need to organize your information. Develop a comps book, and insert the information about the properties you have researched. In addition, gather the information we discussed in Chapter 5 relating to your property (copy of deed, survey, and so forth).

At this point you will also want to get a professional home inspection done to get a punch list of needed repairs to get ready for the clean up and last-minute repairs and renovations to your property. If you are working with a limited budget and you want to do the bare minimum, then use your home inspection as a guide for addressing safety issues and concerns that your home inspector has raised. Studies have shown that one of the big reasons why transactions fall apart is because of latent defects raised by the inspection that were not disclosed to the buyers at the time of negotiations. These will invariably be raised by the buyer's own inspector or real estate maven. The buyer who pays the highest price for a house is the one that has the greatest sense of confidence about the safety and usability of the property. If doubts or questions about the important systems and standards are raised by the buyer or the real estate maven prior to negotiations, this will be a huge stumbling block. For example, improper electrical work often gives the buyer a very uneasy feeling about the safety of the components of a home.

If an unlicensed electrician did electrical work in the house or there are clearly substandard issues like exposed wiring, loose electrical boxes, or faulty switches, these will give the buyers great hesitation in making any offer on the house. The suspicions will spill over into all areas of the house, since the homeowner was careless enough to allow these types of conditions to exist, which are the most dangerous and potentially life-threatening.

Week Two: Clean Up the House and Develop Customer List

In the second week you have two very time-consuming tasks— (1) fixing up and staging your house and (2) developing your buyer's list. Since you have seen your two closest competitors and have seen exactly what they are offering, it is here and now that you can start developing a plan to outdo, out-stage, and out-price your competition. The most important thing you will learn from this book is doing the due diligence and knowing your closest competitors and out-doing them so that you are first in line in getting your house sold.

If you are working with a budget, remember the three most important areas in preparing your house for sale, based on a function of price for effect, are landscaping, carpet (new or cleaned), and paint. Focus your efforts on the entryway, kitchen, and bathrooms. If you are still living the in the house, rent a storage space and clear out at least half of your personal items and furniture. Remove any bulky tables or couches and clear out your closets to make them appear larger. And if you have a small, cramped garage, clear out most of it to make it neat and usable.

In her book *Organize to Be the Best* (Adams Hall, 1991), Susan Silver offers the acronym SPACE to remember what you need to do with your stuff.

S—Sort. Sort out the information into groups.

P—Purge. Get rid of things you don't use.

A—Assign a home. Assign where each item will go in your new home.

C—Containerize. Pack the items into containers.

E—Equalize. Do a little each and every day.

Once your house is renovated, cleaned up, and staged, you are ready to take photos of the house. Remember to pick an overcast day to take the outside shots of the house. Make sure you take pictures from several angles. Crop and edit the photos so that you have most of the house in the frame of the picture. Take shots of the inside using a wide-angle lens. You may need to use a flash and supplemental lighting for the inside shots. If you have a friend who is a camera buff, borrow some flood lighting for the kitchen and bathroom shots.

With your best dozen photos in hand, it's time to design your flyer. Make sure your best photos go first on the front of the flyer in large size, followed by several shots of the kitchen, bathrooms, and other features of your home. Pictures of nearby attractions such as parks, shopping, a golf course, or community pool can also appear on the flyer. Make sure your flyers are in full color and that you have a nice flyer box to display them in front of the house.

You also want to start picking your dates for the upcoming open houses, being mindful of holidays, sporting events, and weather. If you planned ahead, your third week will be the time you start with your first few open houses.

Week Three–Four: Open Houses

Week three is the preparation for your upcoming open houses. Do one final check of the comps to see if any new houses have come on the market or if any of the houses listed for sale have gone under contract. Also, check to see if any of the existing houses have changed prices.

Order your street signs in bulk, at least 100 of them because some will blow away or be removed by your competition. You will want to put out about 20 signs each week, so make sure you have plenty on hand. Mail a postcard on Monday to all of your target customers in the neighborhood so it arrives on Wednesday, giving plenty of time for people to plan on coming to your open house over the weekend. Hire a kid to go door to door with your flyer about the property and the open house. If you are considering working with brokers, mail to the local offices on Tuesday or Wednesday, so that the flyer arrives Thursday or Friday.

Make sure you are prepared for the open house as we discussed in Chapter 8. Get your fish bowl and your sign-in sheets all ready (see

Appendix F for a sample sign-in sheet). Make sure you have all the information about the neighborhood, the schools, and your competition. If you are not using an attorney or a real estate broker, you will need a copy of a real estate contract on hand in case you get someone who is ready to make an offer.

A follow-up system sequencing your buyers in order of name or phone number is important. Software programs such as Microsoft Outlook or ACT! can help you organize a good follow-up system and calendar. If you are computer-phobic, a good old-fashioned index card system and plastic box work just fine. Following up with phone calls to all prospective buyers weekly is the optimum goal. For the most interested buyers, following up and keeping in touch about every two to three days is recommended. If you have a buyer you are in active negotiations with, daily communication is essential.

Weeks Five–Six: Find a Broker

It's been a few weeks, and you've tried selling the property on your own without success; now it's time to pick a real estate broker and get the property on the MLS. As we discussed in Chapter 6, you have to decide whether you will go with a full service broker or a discount broker. If you choose a discount broker or facilitator, you will continue doing the same things—open houses (except in the case of holidays or other big events), mailings to your top prospective leads, and signs around the neighborhood. The only difference now is that you will be getting showings during the week as well.

If you choose to go with a full-service broker, you will start the interview process by finding the top selling agents in your area, as opposed to the top listing agents. Remember, top selling agents are the ones actually doing the selling, whereas listing agents generally get the property sold vicariously through the top selling agents. Sometimes the top listing agent is better than the top selling agent, depending on the overall strength of the agent's recent activity. This can be determined through either an appraiser or an independent third-party real estate broker who can usually identify the most active agents. Interview the top two or three agents or brokers before making your final decision, as described in Chapter 6.

Two to Three Months Later: The Re-Bake or the Round Robin Auction

It's been a few months, and you have used every marketing trick in the book and held several open houses and still no offers. It's time to go back to the book—the comps book. Did you get your ranges right? Did you price your property realistically? Does your house show as well as your competition? Did you do enough marketing? Honest answers to these questions will determine where the weakest links in the chain can be found. Try to talk with as many prospective buyers and brokers as you can so that you can get honest feedback about your house—the good, the bad, and the ugly. Ask friends to tour your house and give you an honest opinion about the property. If your listing has expired, consider a new broker who may put a fresh set of eyes and perspective on the property.

Go research new properties that are under contract, sold, and on the market to see how your competition has evolved. It's possible that the market has changed in the few months since you did you research or that there are new comps on the market. Reconsider the supply quotient and how its rate of change may have affected the overall market values and time on market. We call these steps "getting ahead of the curve." Specifically, as we discussed in Chapter 2, if you marketplace has an increasing supply quotient and its rate of change is significant, then you may have to significantly outprice your competition in order to strike a relatively quick sale.

Consider the re-baked listing as described in Chapter 6. You have two choices in the re-bake. First, you can re-bake the listing with terms. Offering owner financing terms is like completely changing the offer because it's exposing the property to a whole new group of buyers. In fact, those who may have trouble obtaining financing from a traditional source may be willing to pay a higher price because they qualify under the new terms.

Second, you can re-bake the listing with a lower price. If you re-bake your listing, consider taking a new outside photo of the home from a different angle to achieve a different look. Fashion models will often have a photographer take shots from different angles. You should do the same thing with your house.

Re-baking more than once is counterproductive because you start getting into a potentially downward spiral and may end up with a tainted property. If you did your research correctly and priced your property correctly from the beginning, you should have no reason to have to re-bake the listing at a lower price more than once. Instead, consider the round robin auction after you have re-baked the property once and it has not sold in a few months.

Final Thoughts

If you've gotten to this point in the book, congratulations, you've now become an expert on the home seller process in a slow market. If you are a real-estate professional, hopefully you have gotten some nuggets of information that you can use in your real-estate practice. The principles in this book are based on thousands of successful transactions and will work for you if you apply them in the right way, in the proper order, and at the right time.

Selling your house is both a science and an art, so some of what we have discussed in this book will work exactly as we say, and some may have to be adapted for your market and your particular house. Some principles, like negotiating, are universal and will apply to any market, and it is suggested you follow such things by the book.

Studies have shown that most sellers who sell on their own without a broker tend to do so within the first few three weeks. For the persistent sellers who cannot afford to hire a broker, consider using a professional real estate facilitator. The concept of a facilitator is like being your own agent in a real estate office, yet having the support and expertise of the broker/owner at your fingertips. This is an evolutionary process in the industry across the country. You can find more information on facilitators at www.toplocalbroker.com.

Let's keep all this in perspective and remember that at the end of the day you only need one buyer. We have handled literally thousands of real-estate transactions over the last two decades and a very high percentage of them occurred with only one interested buyer. Your job is to do what it takes to not only flush out this buyer, but not to blow up the transaction when he comes knocking on your door. You will only get one shot at doing it right, so make sure you study and apply the principles in this book correctly. We recommend role-playing and practicing with a good friend who has some real estate experience. This same friend should review your marketing materials and the staging of your house to pick up on any obvious flaws that you may have overlooked. Make sure, however, that your friend has read this book!

We wish you the best of success in selling your home quickly and for the highest possible price and welcome your feedback at our web site www.sellyourhousefastbook.com.

Chapter Summary

- Remember your ADOCTORS checklist.
- Plan your attack very methodologically, week by week.

Realtor Supply Products

www.smsproducts.com
www.superiorrealestatesupply.com
www.realestatesupercenter.com
www.sanzospecialties.com
www.reamark.com
www.victorystore.com/realtor
www.realtorstore.biz
www.fmlsstore.com

Custom Vinyl Signs

www.banditsigns.com
www.signsbytomorrow.com
www.speedysigns.com
www.buildasign.com
www.signspecialist.com
www.YardSignWholeSale.com
www.make-realestatesigns.com
www.realestatesigns.com

Color Flier Printing and Photos

www.vistaprint.com
www.printingforless.com
www.printforcolor.com
www.48hourprint.com
www.psprint.com

www.expressflyerprinting.com
www.printplace.com
www.istockphoto.com
www.bigstockphoto.com

Real Estate Flier Templates

www.realflyer.com
www.gururealestateflyers.com
www.expresscopy.com
www.smartdraw.com
www.stocklayouts.com

Real Estate Web Sites

www.listingdomains.com
www.singlepropertywebsite.com
www.nowoffered.com
www.singlepropertysites.com
www.ipropertywebsites.com
www.investorpro.com
www.inetusa.com

For-Sale-by-Owner Web Sites

www.fsbo.com
www.craigslist.org
www.move.com
www.fsbosellbuy.com
www.freerealestateads.net
www.propertytrek.com
www.tcinvestor.com
www.land.net
www.homes-for-sale-by-owner.info
www.fsbofreedom.com
www.fsboguide.com
www.listingpage.com
www.homescape.com
http://realestate.yahoo.com
www.forsalebyowner.com

www.realestatebyowner.com
www.owners.com

For Rent by Owner Web Sites

www.rentals.com
www.move.com
www.rentmarketer.com
www.hotpads.com
www.forrentbyowner.com
http://base.google.com
www.craigslist.org

Furniture Rental

www.cort.com
www.rentacenter.com
www.rentfurniture.com

Virtual Tour Web Sites

www.visualtour.com
www.realtourvision.com
www.360house.com
www.youtube.com

Flat-Fee Brokers

www.iggyshouse.com
www.salebyownerrealty.com
www.flatfeelisting.com
www.valuemls.com
www.fsbo.com

Staging Sites

www.simpleappeal.com
www.homestagingresource.com
www.stagedhomes.com
www.stagetomove.com

www.interiorarrangements.com
www.homestagers.com

Credit Reporting

www.myfico.com
www.annualcreditreport.com
www.freecreditreport.com
www.rentreporters.com
www.equifax.com
www.experian.com
www.transunion.com

Comparable Sales

www.electronicappraiser.com
www.zillow.com
www.dataquick.com
www.sitexdata.com

Telephone Voice Mail and Answering

www.patlive.com
www.gotvmail.com
www.ringcentral.com

Professional Associations and Government Agencies

www.realtor.com	National Association of Realtors
www.ashi.org	American Society of Home Inspectors
www.nachi.org	National Association of Certified Home
www.nahi.org	National Association of Home Inspectors
www.hud.gov	Department of Housing and Urban Development
www.fanniemae.com	Federal National Mortgage Association
www.epa.gov/asbestos	EPA info on asbestos
www.epa.gov/lead	EPA info on lead

Cost of Various Professionals

Attorney	0.5 percent to 2 percent of sales price
Full-service real-estate broker	3 percent to 6 percent of sales price
Flat-fee real-estate listing broker	0 percent to 1 percent of sales price
Buyer's broker	About 3 percent of sales price
Property inspector	$200 to $400
Appraiser	$250 to $500
Structural engineer	$300 to $1,000
Staging professional	0.5 percent to 2 percent of sales price
Title insurance	$500 to $1,500, depending on the price of the home and how long it was owned by the seller
Closing fees	$300 to $1,000, depending on what part of the country

Checklist of Repair/ Replacement Items

	Cost of Materials	Labor Hrs	Totals
Kitchen			
Stainless sink with faucet	100	3.5	
Ceiling light (use same throughout the house)	20	.5	
Counter top with back splash (per ten feet)	75	2	
Cabinet knobs (for 25)	35	2	
Basic electric range (basic model new)	275	2	
Dishwasher (basic model new/nice model used)	250	3	
Bathrooms			
Vanity with faucet	125	3.5	
Toilet with seat	75	2	
Towel bar set	25	.5	
Tub surround kit (replaces worn tile)	75	3	
Medicine cabinet	75	1	
Light fixture	25	.5	
Master Bedroom			
Closet doors (4' unpainted)	65	3	
Ceiling fan with light	50	2	
Door (match existing style)	30	2	
Door knobs (brass set with locks)	15	.25	

(Continued)

Kitchen	Cost of Materials	Labor Hrs	Totals
Floor Coverings (professionally installed per sq ft)			
Sheet Vinyl	2	N/A	
Tile (use 12"×12" neutral colors)	5.0	N/A	
Carpet (with pad)	3.0	N/A	
Other Interior Materials			
Molding (pre-primed per linear foot)	.50	.1	
Interior eggshell paint (per five gallons)	60	8	
Exterior Items			
Exterior flat paint (per five gallons)	75	8	
Exterior light fixture (brass)	25	.5	
Basic single pane window (installed)	100	N/A	
Window screen	25	.5	
Front door	150	3	
Roof shingles (installed) 1,200 sq ft ranch	2,000	N/A	
Front porch stoop repair (including labor)	150	N/A	
Seamless gutters (installed per linear foot)	3	N/A	
Landscape Projects			
New sod (installed per sq ft)	1	N/A	
Juniper Bush (three feet tall per bush)	40	.5	
6' privacy fence (per linear ft, 8' lengths)	10	N/A	
Organic cedar mulch (delivered per cubic yard)	25	.1	

Comps Sheet
Analysis Form

	Comp 1	Comp 2	Comp 3
Sale Price			
Sale Date			
Bedrooms			
Baths			
Sq Ft			
Main Sq Ft			
Basement Sq Ft			
Lot Size			
Special financing			
Special concessions			
School district			
Garage			
Condition of yard			
Curb appeal			
A/C			
Age of house			
Updated?			
Location			

Staging Checklist

- ❑ Remove clutter
- ❑ Clean yard
- ❑ Clean windows
- ❑ Empty out closets
- ❑ Empty out garage
- ❑ Replace all light bulbs
- ❑ Paint front door bold color
- ❑ Make doorway inviting—plants, doormat, and so forth
- ❑ Make foyer inviting—table, flowers, welcome info, door mat
- ❑ Remove all screens
- ❑ Scents and sounds—candles and music
- ❑ Paint walls
- ❑ Clean or replace appliances
- ❑ Decorate kitchen and baths
- ❑ Re-arrange furniture
- ❑ Add or remove wall décor
- ❑ Add or remove rugs
- ❑ Clean carpets
- ❑ Add landscaping
- ❑ Clean basement and window wells

Sample Ads and Signs for Lease/Option or Owner Financing

Newspaper Signs

RENT-TO-OWN!

Excellent oppty to own your own home! 3 br, 2 ba, near airport. Low dwn payment and $1500/month. 555-5555

OWNER WILL
FINANCE
3 BR HOUSE
303-444-1111

LEASE/PURCHASE!

Build equity while U rent! 3br, 2ba near school, $1500/month plus small dwn payment. 555-5555

RENT-TO-OWN!

Build equity while U rent! 3br, 2ba near school. $1500/month plus small dwn payment. 555-5555

NO CREDIT REQUIRED OWNER WILL FINANCE

Excellent oppty to own your own home! Small down payment. 555-5555

Open House Sign-in Sheet

Name	Address	Home Phone	Cell Phone	When Are You Looking to Move?

Round Robin Bid Sheet—Cash Sale

Name	Address	Home Phone	Cell Phone	Price

Round Robin Bid Sheet– Owner Financed Sale

Name	Address	Home Phone	Cell Phone	Down Pmt/Price

State-by-State List of Commonly Used Security Lien

State	Security Commonly Used
Alabama	Mortgage
Alaska	Deed of Trust
Arizona	Deed of Trust
Arkansas	Deed of Trust
California	Deed of Trust
Colorado	Deed of Trust
Connecticut	Mortgage
Delaware	Mortgage
District of Columbia	Deed of Trust
Florida	Mortgage
Georgia	Mortgage
Hawaii	Mortgage
Idaho	Deed of Trust
Illinois	Mortgage
Indiana	Mortgage
Iowa	Mortgage
Kansas	Mortgage
Kentucky	Mortgage and Deed of Trust
Louisiana	Mortgage
Maine	Mortgage
Maryland	Deed of Trust
Massachusetts	Mortgage
Michigan	Mortgage
Minnesota	Mortgage

(Continued)

State	Security Commonly Used
Mississippi	Deed of Trust
Missouri	Deed of Trust
Montana	Deed of Trust
Nebraska	Deed of Trust
Nevada	Deed of Trust
New Hampshire	Mortgage
New Jersey	Mortgage
New Mexico	Mortgage
New York	Mortgage
North Carolina	Deed of Trust
North Dakota	North Dakota
Ohio	Mortgage
Oklahoma	Mortgage
Oregon	Deed of Trust
Pennsylvania	Mortgage
Rhode Island	Mortgage
South Carolina	Mortgage
South Dakota	Mortgage
Tennessee	Deed of Trust
Texas	Deed of Trust
Utah	Deed of Trust
Vermont	Mortgage
Virginia	Deed of Trust
Washington	Deed of Trust
West Virginia	Deed of Trust
Wisconsin	Mortgage
Wyoming	Mortgage